Discover how the gems of Islam can help you along your path, no matter what your spiritual practice.

"In this world, no matter what plans we make or things we acquire, the thief will come from the unguarded side. Be occupied, then, with your inner life. It is a gift of real and lasting value."

—FROM THE INTRODUCTION

Drawing on the foundational texts of Islamic spirituality—the Qur'an, sayings of the Prophet Muhammad and wisdom teaching stories—and with Imam Jamal Rahman as your guide, you will:

+ Explore the mysteries of the Qur'an, the purpose of life and God
+ Delve into the essential work of transforming your ego
+ Exercise the spiritual practices of prayer and remembrance of God
+ Celebrate diversity, drawing on Qur'anic revelation to "come to know each other"
+ Learn how authentic community and practicing justice can contribute to your faith
+ Become present with the mysteries of the invisible world
+ And much more ...

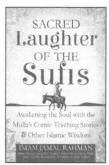
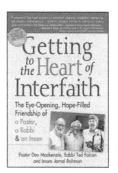
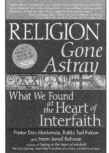

IMAM JAMAL RAHMAN, a popular speaker on Islam, Sufi spirituality and interfaith relations, has been featured in the *New York Times*, on *CBS News*, the BBC and various NPR programs. Co-founder and Muslim Sufi minister at Interfaith Community Church and adjunct faculty at Seattle University, he is a former host of Interfaith Talk Radio and travels nationally and internationally, presenting at retreats and workshops. He is co-author of *Getting to the Heart of Interfaith: The Eye-Opening, Hope-Filled Friendship of a Pastor, a Rabbi & an Imam* and *Religion Gone Astray: What We Found at the Heart of Interfaith*, and author of *Sacred Laughter of the Sufis: Awakening the Soul with the Mulla's Comic Teaching Stories & Other Islamic Wisdom* (all SkyLight Paths) and *The Fragrance of Faith: The Enlightened Heart of Islam*, among other books.

"A gem all its own ... a wonderful guidebook to spiritual living.... Allows the Qur'an to speak beyond the boundaries of Islam."
—RAMI SHAPIRO, author, *The Sacred Art of Lovingkindness: Preparing to Practice*

"Beautiful ... reaches deep into the heart and soul, reminding us of our divine nature. Allow its deep Qur'anic wisdom to guide you on your journey Home."
—LLEWELLYN VAUGHAN-LEE, PhD, Sufi teacher; author, *Prayer of the Heart in Christian and Sufi Mysticism*

"A modern-day jewel of some of the richest offerings of Islam.... Goes to the very depth of the rich oceans of Islamic spirituality to bring us pearls of wisdom and beauty."
—OMID SAFI, professor of Islamic studies, University of North Carolina at Chapel Hill; author, *Memories of Muhammad*

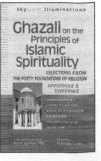

SPIRITUAL GEMS *of* ISLAM

Insights & Practices from the Qur'an, Hadith, Rumi & Muslim Teaching Stories to Enlighten the Heart & Mind

IMAM JAMAL RAHMAN

Walking Together, Finding the Way®
SKYLIGHT PATHS®
PUBLISHING

Spiritual Gems of Islam:
Insights & Practices from the Qur'an, Hadith, Rumi & Muslim Teaching Stories to
Enlighten the Heart & Mind

© 2013 by Jamal Rahman

Library of Congress Cataloging-in-Publication Data

Rahman, Jamal.
 Spiritual gems of islam : insights & practices from the qur'an, hadith, rumi & muslim teaching stories to enlighten the heart & mind / By Imam Jamal Rahman.
   p. cm.
 Includes bibliographical references and index.
 ISBN 978-1-59473-430-4 (alk. paper)
 1. Islam—Quotations, maxims, etc. 2. Spiritual life—slam. 3. Islamic ethics. I. Title.
 BP161.3.R34 2013
 297.5'7—dc23
                          2013003056

ISBN 978-1-59473-527-1 (eBook)
ISBN 978-1-68336-310-1 (hc)

Manufactured in the United States of America
Cover Art: © Philip Lange/iStockphoto.com
Cover Design: Jenny Buono
Interior Design: Kelley Barton

SkyLight Paths Publishing is creating a place where people of different spiritual traditions come together for challenge and inspiration, a place where we can help each other understand the mystery that lies at the heart of our existence.

SkyLight Paths sees both believers and seekers as a community that increasingly transcends traditional boundaries of religion and denomination—people wanting to learn from each other, *walking together, finding the way.*

Walking Together, Finding the Way
Published by SkyLight Paths Publishing
www.skylightpaths.com

Dedicated to the memory of my beloved parents,
Ataur and Suraiya Rahman,
who were my most treasured teachers.

CONTENTS

PURIFYING AND EXPANDING THE HEART

REMEMBERING YOUR SUSTAINER

DOING WHAT IS BEAUTIFUL

WALKING ON SPACIOUS PATHS

BEING IN THE MYSTERY

INTRODUCTION

WE HUMANS SEEM TO HAVE A UNIVERSAL NEED TO understand and describe our sojourn on Earth. This need has given rise to many spiritual paths and countless metaphors over the millennia. Out of this boundless supply of metaphors, two favorites guide my personal journey and provide the foundation for this book.

The first is a Qur'anic verse about spaciousness: "God has made the Earth a wide expanse for you so that you may walk thereon on spacious paths" (71:20). From my beloved parents, as well as from Islamic sages and Sufi mystics, I have learned that walking those spacious paths means walking softly and humbly on Earth, giving freely of what we love, and striving to transform an enemy into a friend. These are not the musings of a poet; they are Qur'anic injunctions from God. But this prescribed outer spaciousness is impossible to accomplish unless we acquire an inner spaciousness, an inner capacity to encompass our joys, sorrows, anger, paradoxes, and bewilderment in a manner that opens our hearts to the oneness of all creation. This inner work is also a path, according to the Holy Book, and while it may ultimately be spacious, at the beginning it can be steep and difficult. Once we awaken to the reality of our higher self, our first tentative steps along the path will grow ever stronger and more certain as we engage in the lifelong process of freeing the ego from its self-attachment and surrendering to the Divinity at the core of our being.

And how shall we accomplish this lofty goal? This is the subject of my other favorite metaphor: The sages say we must polish our hearts and minds as if they were rubies in the rough. For our divine ruby light to shine from within, we must continue and never cease the work of refining all facets of our intellect and heart. If we stop polishing because we get irritated by every rub, how will we ever smooth our rough edges?[1]

Tapping the Wellspring of Islamic Spirituality

No matter what metaphor we use, there is no escaping the stark truth that to live a meaningful life—one that brings us joy, contentment, and fulfillment—we have to do the inner spiritual work of becoming a more complete human being. This book is a practical guide for spiritual seekers of any religion, or none, who wish to live life with the awareness and intentionality that can come from perennial wisdom and insight. There are, of course, many spiritual paths open to sincere seekers, but closest to my heart, because it is the religion of my birth, is the wellspring of Islamic spirituality. Over the centuries, Islamic sages have gleaned timeless spiritual insights and practices from sacred texts, meditation, and knowledge of the heart. These have been passed down from generation to generation, and I invite you to use this wisdom to nurture and nourish your own spiritual path.

Regardless of where you are on your spiritual journey—whether you are already committed to it or are just beginning to think about it—this book will be helpful to you. If you are on a path that you believe is the only way to find God, you may be moved to find that countless others are seeking the same personal goal of salvation, freedom, or surrender via other steep paths and they may even have some climbing tips for you. If you are rooted in your own tradition but open to learning about the beauty and wisdom of others, you may discover insights that deepen your love of your own tradition as well as your appreciation of fellow travelers on different paths. If you are one of the many who say, "I'm spiritual but not religious," the metaphor of bees collecting nectar from a variety of flowers may resonate for you. And even if you are firm in agnosticism or atheism, at the very least you may find that many of the reflections and practices will nourish your being and help you become a more centered and complete individual.

Spiritual Nourishment

"To God belong the most beautiful names," says the Qur'an (59:24), and according to Islamic tradition, the divine names number ninety-nine. Any factor of ninety-nine is said to be graced by a mysterious sacredness. Thus, this book is a series of contemplations on thirty-three gems of Islamic spirituality: a personal choice of verses of beauty and wisdom from the Qur'an, sayings of the Prophet Muhammad, and the works of Sufi poets, especially the thirteenth-century mystic Jelaluddin Rumi. Also woven into the contemplations are teaching stories, especially those of Mulla Nasruddin, Islam's great comic foil. Some include vignettes drawn from my life and work.

The outline of the thirty-three gems is as follows:

Gems 1–4 introduce us to the mysteries of the Qur'an, the purpose of life, and God.

Gems 5–11 delve into the essential inner work of transforming the ego, and cultivating compassion and awareness.

Gems 12–16 continue the inner work of purifying and expanding the heart, and surrendering to divine will.

Gems 17–18 explain the spiritual practices of prayer and remembrance of God.

Gems 19–26 elaborate on the need to do what is beautiful: participate in righteous deeds, create authentic community, practice justice, maintain balance, and deepen one's faith.

Gems 27–29 encourage us to walk on spacious paths by helping us to overcome gender bias, celebrate diversity, get to know the other, and learn to forgive.

Gems 30–33 ask us to be present with the mysteries of the invisible world, death, and the afterlife.

Qur'an, Hadith, and Rumi

Qur'anic translations are primarily from *The Meaning of the Holy Qur'an,* translated by Yusuf Ali. Other translations used are from *The Message of the Qur'an,* by Muhammad Asad, and *The Light of Dawn: Daily Readings from the Holy Qur'an,* by Camille Helminski. These books are listed in the Bibliography.

In the history of Islam, there were many scholars who collected sayings of the Prophet Muhammad (hadith in Arabic). Hadith are the Prophet's own words, and hadith qudsi are God's words communicated to the Prophet, usually through a dream. Since all these collections are based on hearsay, it is hard to verify which ones are genuine. According to many Islamic scholars, there are six collectors, all from the ninth century, whose collections are diligent and meticulous, and, therefore, they are considered more authentic than others. They are as follows:

Sahih al-Bukhari, collected by Imam Bukhari (d. 870)

Sahih Muslim, collected by Imam Muslim (d. 875)

Sunan an-Nasa'i, collected by Imam Nasa'i (d. 915)

Sunnan Abu Dawud, collected by Imam Abu Dawud (d. 888)

Sunnan al-Tirmidhi, collected by Imam Tirmidhi (d. 892)

Sunnan Ibn Maja, collected by Imam Ibn Maja (d. 886)

Most of the hadith quoted in this book come from one of the six authentic collections listed above and are not individually cited. Only when a hadith is drawn from outside of these collections is attribution included in the text.

Besides Qur'anic verses and hadith, I have included in my chapters brief utterances by the thirteenth-century sage Rumi. These are based on translations of Rumi by Kabir and Camille Helminski and Coleman Barks. The books I have used are listed below:

> *Jewels of Remembrance: A Daybook of Spiritual Guidance Containing 365 Selections from the Wisdom of Rumi,* by Kabir and Camille Helminski
>
> *Rumi: Daylight—A Daybook of Spiritual Guidance,* by Kabir and Camille Helminski
>
> *The Essential Rumi,* by Coleman Barks

In a few instances I have used sayings from the fourteenth-century poet Hafiz. The translations are by Daniel Ladinsky from his books titled *The Gift* and *Love Poems to God.* A complete listing of these books is found in the Bibliography.

Also, I have sometimes included traditional Sufi sayings that have been transmitted orally from generation to generation. I heard them from my parents, who heard them from their parents.

Sufism: Essence over Form

A question I am often asked is, "What is a Sufi?" Sufis are Muslims who emphasize essence over form and substance over appearance in their spiritual practices. If the institution of religion can be compared to a cup and the water in it is the spiritual message, Sufis lament that we spend too much time polishing the outside of the cup and neglect to drink the water. They do subscribe to outer rituals, but are mostly eager to do the inner work. They aspire to taste and live the essence of their faith. To give an example of the Sufi approach to teachings, a conservative Islamic theologian might say that a Muslim who does not perform the five cycles of daily prayers will suffer punishment in the hereafter. A Sufi teacher, on the other hand, will liken prayers to attendance at celestial banquets. A practitioner who fails to pray is missing out on the joy of the feast. That loss is the punishment.

Sufism is not a denomination in Islam. The two main denominations are Sunni (85 percent) and Shia (15 percent). The differences between Shia and Sunni are rooted in a historical dispute about the choice of a community leader after the death of the Prophet in 632 CE. Although both denominations share the same fundamental articles of faith, their historical conflict has created differences in forms of practices, which, to some, are significant. There are both Sunni and Shia Sufis. It is generally accepted that the spiritual beauty of Sufi teachings is largely responsible for the spread of Islam in South, Southeast, and Central Asia, where the majority of Muslims live, and in China, Russia, Europe, and parts of Africa.

Can a non-Muslim be a Sufi? Sufi teachers reply yes, and explain their answer with a metaphor. Muslims point their prayer rugs in the direction of the Kabah[2] in Mecca. What happens if they become enlightened and find themselves praying inside the Kabah? In that state, does it matter in what direction the prayer rug is pointing?

Teaching Stories and Insights of the Mulla

There is an ancient Sufi saying that a precious gold coin can sometimes be recovered with the help of a penny candle, meaning that sometimes the profoundest truths are best illuminated through simple stories. A time-honored Sufi practice is to meditate on teaching stories that expand the mind and heart in order to fathom the depths of sacred texts. I was fortunate to be introduced at an early age to the legendary stories of the Mulla, Islam's great comic foil. Timeless and placeless, the mythical Mulla is a village simpleton and sage rolled into one. He has no image to cling to and no reputation to uphold.

He enjoys laughing at himself and invites us to join him. Even though he has no formal education, he is given the title of *Mulla*, which indicates a person of some learning. A favorite portrait of the Mulla is that of a middle-aged man, dressed in turban and cloak, seated on a donkey and rushing through the marketplace. When the townsfolk hail him, he replies hastily, "Sorry, I can't stop to talk. I'm looking for my donkey!"

The Mulla's wisdom seems to emanate from a source beyond book learning. Just as each verse of the Qur'an has several levels of meaning, so does every Mulla story. For example, one story pokes fun at the complexity and absurdity of human nature. The Mulla, in deep exasperation, sought a cure from a healer because every night for the past month he had dreamt about having wrestling matches with donkeys. The healer thoughtfully prepared a special herbal mixture for him and said, "Eat this, and your dreams will go away." "Thank you so much, but can I start tomorrow?" the Mulla asked. "Why not tonight?" the healer inquired. Said the Mulla, "Because tonight I am scheduled to wrestle in the finals of the championship match!"

Clerics who go to absurd lengths to defend institutions that have become corrupted also come in for their share of playful ridicule. One rainy evening, the Mulla attended a religious meeting in a house of worship. As the leader was declaiming about the beauty and superiority of their particular institution, a fierce storm arose and the weak rafters of the sacred house began to creak ominously. "Don't worry," said the leader. "These rafters are actually singing hymns of praise out of love for God." Hearing this, the Mulla pointed toward the swaying rafters and asked, "But what if the building, out of love for God, decides to bow and prostrate itself to the Almighty?"

In Turkey, there is a tomb of the famous Mulla. In the front is a secure iron door with chains and padlocks, but no walls surround the door. Even in his tomb, the Mulla offers us a teaching: In this world, no matter what plans we make or things we acquire, the thief will come from the unguarded side. Be occupied, then, with your inner life. It is a gift of real and lasting value.

Practical Guidance

Each gem, or chapter in this book, has a particular theme and ends with discussion questions and at least one spiritual practice. Some discussion questions are preceded by verses or sayings to reflect upon. Each gem is self-contained, and it is not necessary to read the book in a linear fashion. However, it is best to read these gems little by little. Too many insights, verses, teaching stories, and practices all at once can cause spiritual indigestion.

My prayer is that these timeless spiritual gems will illuminate your chosen path and, by grace of God, provide joy and practical guidance for your personal journey into the fullness of your sacred being.

God's Gender

While the Qur'an refers to God, or Allah, using the masculine gender—He, His, Him—Islam embraces both genders in its conception of God. In quoting the Qur'an, this book sometimes uses male pronouns, reflecting this convention.

OPENING UP
TO THE
LIGHT

"This Is the Book"

(QUR'AN 2:2)

"Meditate on Its Signs"

(QUR'AN 38:29)

The Qur'an's Timeless Spiritual Guidance

For nearly a quarter of the Earth's population, the primary source of spiritual wisdom is the Holy Qur'an, a wellspring of guidance, discernment, remembrance, and mercy delivered to the Prophet Muhammad in Arabia fourteen hundred years ago. According to Islamic tradition, in the early hours of a morning in the year 610 CE, as Muhammad—not yet a prophet—was meditating in a mountain cave near Mecca, a blinding light appeared, announced itself as angel Gabriel, and ordered Muhammad to "Proclaim! [or Recite!] in the name of thy Lord and Cherisher" (96:1). Gripped with fear, Muhammad bolted from the cave and ran down the mountain into the loving embrace of his wife, Khadija, who comforted him and reassured him that he wasn't losing his mind. Then, after consulting a Christian seer who recognized that something truly divine was happening, Khadija persuaded Muhammad to return to the cave. Once again, the luminous angel appeared and commanded him to recite. This time, Muhammad felt an unbearable pressure, as if he were being squeezed, and from his lips poured out words of such exquisite beauty that they were seared into his soul. Upon returning home he repeated them to his family and close companions, who faithfully wrote them down word for word. To this day, the occasion of his first encounter with the angel Gabriel has been known and celebrated in Islam as the Night of Power. The mysterious transmissions continued intermittently for twenty-three years, and the revelations eventually were codified into a book of 114 chapters known as the Qur'an, which means "recitation."

The Qur'anic recitations were delivered in a style of Arabic that linguistic scholars say is unsurpassed in literary beauty. The sounds of the words penetrate the Muslim body and soul even before they reach the mind. As a child I loved to recite from the Qur'an because I was told that God hides in its verses so that, as you recite them, God can kiss your lips. As an adolescent I learned from my parents how to study the Qur'an and search out its hidden meanings with the guidance of the thirteenth-century mystic Jelaluddin Rumi, who called himself a servant of the Qur'an. Now, with graying hair, I have come to the realization that I will never plumb the depths of the Holy Book in this lifetime.

Every verse is also called a sign, and we are called to "meditate on its signs" (38:29) so that we may grow in understanding of the Holy One who seems to hide in plain sight in the readily accessible verses but reveals Himself most sweetly in the mysterious ones. Only those "willing to take it to heart" (54:17) can understand the radiant truths and secret meaning in the signs. "None save God knows its final meaning" (3:7), the Holy Book says, but sages tell us that if we truly listen, the spiritual verses will provide specific signs to each of us about how to become fully human and conscious of God, and about how to live in community and offer our beings in service to God's creation.

In addition to being a primary source of timeless spiritual guidance, the Qur'an is also a compendium of rules and regulations. The Holy Book is said to cover "everything from the sun to the moth,"[1] but mostly it covers a vast range of legal topics, such as inheritance, money lending, marriage, divorce, ethics, and social justice. It is this legal compendium that presents a problem for many modern readers, for while the general principles of justice and ethics are as timeless as the spiritual ones, a few verses particular to that time and place—seventh-century Arabia—seem to foster religious exclusivity, violence, unequal treatment of women, and prejudice against homosexuals. I have addressed these verses in some detail in a book with my Interfaith Amigos, Rabbi Ted Falcon and Pastor Don Mackenzie, called *Religion Gone Astray* (SkyLight Paths). Although such verses are open to interpretation and contextual explanation, we also need to acknowledge that they are not fully consistent with the overall message of the Qur'an. If we believe that every single verse is divine *and timeless*, then any interpretation of the difficult verses must emanate from our higher self and not from our shadow side. Spiritual teachers say that interpretation of any scriptural verse depends on the consciousness and intention of the person. As Rumi reminds us, a bee and a wasp may drink from the same flower, but one produces nectar and the other a sting. We must choose the nectar.

In order to more fully understand some of the signs or different levels of meaning in the verses of the Qur'an, Muslims also turn to the life and collected sayings of the Prophet, teachings of spiritual masters, and the inner knowledge of their own hearts.

Muhammad's Story: Reading the Signs of Silence and Space

The story of the Prophet's life evokes exquisite tenderness in the hearts of Muslims. Orphaned at the age of six, Muhammad possessed a mystical bent of mind and, from an early age, spent time in silence in the Meccan caves, often for forty days and nights at a time. After his experience of the Night of Power, the Prophet preached the Oneness of God and advocated tirelessly for the marginalized and dispossessed. Amazingly, he was able to break with the centuries-old cultural traditions and religious practices of the seventh-century Arabian tribes who idolized wealth and power. When tribal members tried to dissuade him from his mission and belief, he said he would never relent "even if you put the Sun in my right hand and the Moon in my left hand."[2] Harassed, persecuted, and targeted for assassination in Mecca, the Prophet received an unexpected invitation from tribal leaders in Yathrib (now known as Medina, in western Saudi Arabia) to serve as their leader. In 622 CE, he made the shift, or *hijra*, from Mecca to Medina. In the ensuing ten short years of his life, the Prophet was able to unite the warring tribes into one community and lay the groundwork for Islam to become a world civilization and religion. Because of his incredible accomplishments, and even more because of his vision, mercy, and courage, Muslims have the utmost admiration and heartfelt affection for him.

Just as we are told to meditate on the signs in the Qur'an, we may well meditate on the valuable signs in the story of the Prophet and the revelation of the Holy Book. First, Muhammad's experience in the Meccan cave is a sign of divine Presence and power in the mystery of silence. Sages say that silence is the language of God; everything else is a poor translation. Then, his ability to break out of the rigid molds of his tribal conditioning and even, eventually, transform the tribe into a community of believers is a sign that we too can transcend our conditioning and transform our egos so that we may, from a place of inner spaciousness, serve the God of all of humanity. Then there is the sign of the Prophet's *hijra*, his relocation from Mecca to Medina, which provided the safety and what we may call "space" to develop his fledgling faith and community. Like Muhammad, we may need a personal *hijra*—whether a spiritual shift or a physical relocation—to transform our lives. So significant was Muhammad's *hijra* in the birth of Islam that Muslims count the years from the time of the *hijra* in 622 CE, which is year 1 in the Islamic calendar.

Hadith, Teachers, and Individual Understanding

To fully grasp the meaning of the Qur'an, Muhammad's followers were naturally keen to record and share nearly everything the Prophet said and did, and eventually scholars began collecting his sayings (hadith) and stories about his life and conduct (*sunnah*). Some scholars were meticulous and methodical about establishing the authenticity of these reports, carefully examining both their content and the chain of narration. Unfortunately, an alarmingly large number of false and fabricated hadith have crept into Islamic traditions and culture. Muslims are cautioned to take to heart only those hadith that conform to the core teachings of the Qur'an. It is reported that the Prophet himself said, "Compare what purports to come from me with the book of God. What agrees with it, I have said; what disagrees with, I have not said." The renowned fourteenth-century historian Ibn Khaldun asks Muslims to reject any hadith "which differs from the common sense meaning of the Qur'an, no matter how trustworthy the narrators may have been."[3] Because, in theory, Islam does not subscribe to religious hierarchy, ordained ministry, or official priesthood, teachers play a prominent role in developing and explaining spiritual guidance in the Qur'an. Islamic history abounds with spiritual teachers, especially in the millennium after the Prophet's death. Just as it is wise to consult the experts before attempting to climb a mountain, so it is important to consult spiritual teachers or guides from time to time as we climb what the Qur'an calls "the path that is steep" (90:11). The ultimate guide, however, is our own inner teacher. In the words of a traditional saying, "The teacher kindles the light; the oil is already in the lamp."

Individual reasoning, in the context of Islamic spirituality, refers to consultation with the knowledge in one's heart. The word *heart* is mentioned 132 times in the Qur'an and a hadith qudsi states that God resides in the purified human heart. When we work to purify ourselves and remove what the Qur'an calls the innermost dross of the heart, our human heart is graced with access to divine light and wisdom. So important and trustworthy is the heart's inner knowledge that the Prophet advised, "Even if the religious judge advises you about earthly matters, first consult your heart."

Principles and Pillars of Islam

The Prophet Muhammad took to heart some of the signs embedded in the divine revelations and from them derived the three principles and five pillars of Islam. These constitute the core of Islamic spirituality. A hadith relates that an enigmatic person dressed in white appeared out of nowhere to the Prophet and his companions. In a brief conversation he confirmed to the Prophet that the truth of his understanding about the principles and pillars was sound. The person dressed in white disappeared as mysteriously as he arrived. To his astonished companions, the Prophet confided that the visitor was the angel Gabriel.

The first principle is *Islam,* which means "surrender in peace." What we are surrendering is attachment to our ego so that there is space for God in the center of our lives. Sooner or later, circumstances in life will make us realize that "Truly, my prayer and my service of sacrifice, my life and my death are [all] for Allah, the Cherisher of the Worlds" (6:162). The second principle is faith—primarily faith in God, angels, prophets, holy books, and the Day of Judgment. To deepen faith, explains the Qur'an, we have to move from hearsay to inner witnessing to inner certainty (102:5, 102:7, 69:51). Mere belief will not suffice. Teachers call it moving from "borrowed certainty" to "inner certainty." The third principle is beautification of oneself with the divine attributes of God. "Who has a better dye than God?" asks the Qur'an (2:138). The sign of a developed human being—a *wali,* or friend of God—is profound courtesy of the heart known as *adab.* It is said that the primary characteristics of a *wali* are graciousness and generosity.

The first pillar of Islam is the two-part profession of faith known as the *shahada:* "There is no god but God, and Muhammad is a Messenger of God." The first part is best explained by Qur'anic verses testifying to the omnipresence and eternity of God: "Everywhere you turn is the Face of Allah" (2:115); "We are closer to you than your jugular vein" (50:16); "All that is on Earth will perish but forever will abide the Face of your Sustainer, full of Majesty and Abundant

Honor" (55:26–27). The second part of the *shahada* acknowledges Muhammad's pivotal role as a conduit for the Qur'an and founder of the Islamic faith.

The second pillar of Islam is prayer. The Qur'an says, "All that is in the Heavens and all that is on Earth extols the limitless glory of God" (62:1). Several times a day Muslims bow and prostrate themselves to God, an act that deepens intimacy between the devotee and God. The joy of this closeness caused the Prophet to declare, "The freshness of my eyes is given to me in prayer."

The third pillar is charity, which involves giving "freely of what you love" (3:92) and helping the marginalized.

The fourth pillar is Ramadan, which refers to the spiritual practice of abstaining from food, drink, and sexual activity from dawn to dusk during the ninth month of the Islamic lunar calendar. It was during this month that the Night of Power occurred, and the Ramadan fast is an expression of gratitude for the gift of the Qur'an as well as a time of self-purification so that we might remain conscious of God (2:183).

The fifth pillar of Islam is Hajj, the pilgrimage to Mecca in the twelfth month of the Islamic calendar. Able-bodied Muslims who can afford it are expected to go on Hajj at least once in their lives "in the service of Allah" (2:196). Joining fellow Muslims from all over the world in the rituals of the Hajj is a glorious reminder of the importance and sacredness of a community of faith as we live out our lifelong pilgrimage from this world to the next.

REFLECTIONS
AND
PRACTICE

From "Selected Qur'anic Passages and Hadith" (page 216), choose at least one Qur'anic verse that could serve as a guide or inspiration for the next few days. Why does the verse appeal to you?

In the course of the day, repeat the verse in your heart. Reflect on it from time to time. Allow it to percolate in you. Notice whether you experience alignments in your speech and behavior in your highest interest.

"The Qur'an Is a Shy and Veiled Bride"

(RUMI)

Enlisting Friends for the Journey

I usually advise my non-Muslim friends who are interested in Islamic spirituality not to rush out and buy a translation of the Qur'an. For a variety of reasons, the Holy Book might come across as confusing and bewildering. The Qur'an is a "recitation" and its Arabic words are meant to be recited and heard. Divine revelations in the original Arabic possess distinctive rhythms, impassioned cadences, dramatic rumblings, and mysterious oaths and adjurations that stir the soul even before the actual meaning reaches the brain. According to tradition, the angel Gabriel advised the Prophet on the order of the chapters and verses for optimal impact of divine sounds and insights. Thus, the arrangement of the Qur'an is neither linear nor chronological. The verses are not organized from the first revelation that descended on the Prophet to the last one he received. In fact, the first verses uttered by the Prophet in the Meccan cave appear in chapter 96. Also, the spiritual verses in the Qur'an are interspersed with social rules and regulations as well as comments on events of seventh-century Arabia. In the first attempt to read the Qur'an for spiritual insights, it is helpful to choose a book that contains just annotated selections, and to read it in tandem with the writings of an Islamic mystic who has spent a lifetime gleaning the inner meanings of the Holy Book. The Qur'an is like a shy and veiled bride, says Rumi in his short collection of discourses, *Fihi ma Fihi* (It Is What It Is), and we are advised not to approach her directly but to enlist the help of her friends. Friends are the sages and mystics who abound in Islam. Choose an Islamic mystic who appeals to your sensibilities (the most popular ones in the West are Rumi, Hafiz, and Ibn Arabi), and prepare gradually to meet the bride.

My own "best friend" for approaching the Qur'an is Rumi, the writings of whom I first encountered during my formative years when my parents were posted as diplomats to Iran and Turkey, where Rumi is especially revered. Born in Afghanistan in 1207, this Persian sage spent most of his life in Turkey. He was a child prodigy following in the footsteps of his learned father, whom he succeeded as a professor of the Qur'an and Islamic sciences. The brilliance of his mind and the breadth of his scholarship brought him fame, respectability, and many admiring students in the university town of Konya. Then a midlife encounter with an eccentric holy man named Shams of Tabriz turned his world upside down. This meeting is considered a pivotal episode in the history of Islamic spirituality.

Not much is known about Shams of Tabriz. Some sources describe him as a "knower of divine secrets" who was directed by God to travel in the direction of Konya, where Rumi resided. In a popular version of the encounter, Rumi was sitting by a fountain, poring over valuable manuscripts with his doting students, when Shams burst into the courtyard and shouted, "What is all this studying and studying?!" Offended by the rude interruption, Rumi sarcastically replied, "You wouldn't understand." Suddenly, Shams grabbed the manuscripts and tossed them into the fountain. Aghast, Rumi rushed to retrieve the documents, but Shams stopped him and began taking out the papers one by one. Amazingly, each page turned bone-dry as he touched it, and the astonished Rumi exclaimed, "What is this?!" Retorted Shams, "You wouldn't understand!" That encounter led to a remarkable friendship. Shams of Tabriz, the knower of divine secrets, and Rumi, friend of God, were inseparable for many months as Shams communicated his secrets and Rumi was transformed from scholar to ecstatic friend of the Beloved. In trancelike states, Rumi began uttering words of astonishing beauty and wisdom, which were recorded by scribes over several years and put into book form. There were approximately seventy thousand verses in all. Then, as suddenly as he appeared, Shams disappeared. To cope with his pain and distress over the loss of his mentor and friend Rumi began to whirl and turn around his heart, with arms outstretched, a practice that took him to inner states beyond joy or sorrow. This is the origin of his spiritual order of whirling dervishes.

Rumi's message is simple but marvelously enchanting and hopeful: If he, stuck in the mental layers of his mind, was able to break open his heart, so could we. He wants us to taste the unreserved joy of morphing into more complete human beings, as he did. His utterances and metaphors describe the inner alchemy and amazing possibilities: An ordinary stick turns into a flower bud, ground becomes green in a spring wind, a stone is transformed into a ruby. Rumi says that he burst through the "seven worlds"— referring to the seven levels of Heaven the Prophet Muhammad ascended in his night journey called the *lailat al miraj* (see Gem 17), but also referring to higher states of consciousness—and we can, too. With sincerity and fervent enthusiasm he reminds us, "This is in your power."

As precious as Rumi's words and insights about the inner meaning of the Qur'an are to us, even more inspiring is the fact that they arose not from scholarship alone but from his life's work to transform his ego and expand his heart. "I am a slave of the Qur'an," he said. "I am dust on the path of Muhammad."[1] The sage meticulously undertook all the spiritual practices suggested by the Qur'an, which were also modeled by the Prophet Muhammad. From a place of inner knowing, Rumi has important advice about our motives for approaching that "shy bride," the Qur'an. We should not try to unveil her just to satisfy our curiosity about her beauty. Rather, our work is to ensure that we ourselves are beautiful by purifying our hearts and offering ourselves in service to others. Then, when we approach her, she will voluntarily remove her veil and we will behold her beauty in all its radiance.

REFLECTIONS
AND
PRACTICE

From the life of the Prophet Muhammad (or any other prophet with whom you are familiar), choose a spiritual practice that you would like to try for at least a month. For example, like the Prophet, you might meditate regularly in a quiet, secluded place, or fast one day a week, or pray at least once a day. How does your sustained adoption of this practice enhance your understanding of your sacred text?

"I Was a Secret Treasure and I Longed to Be Known"

(HADITH QUDSI)

RUMI, THE BELOVED POET AND MYSTIC FROM THIRTEENTH-century Persia, says that we arrive on Earth a little bit "tipsy." Mulla Nasruddin, the comedic antihero of countless teaching stories, would agree. In one of these stories, the Mulla spends a long evening at the local tavern. Finally, in the early hours of the morning, he stumbles out of the tavern intoxicated[1] and walks the streets aimlessly. A policeman accosts him and asks, "What are you doing here at this hour? Who are you? Where did you come from? And where are you going?" The Mulla replies, "Sir, if I knew the answers to all those questions, I'd be home already!"

Little do we know who we are, where we come from, and where we are going. As we go through the stages of life, we are baffled by things we hear about God, death, and the afterlife. "The lover visible, the Beloved invisible, whose crazy idea was this?" asks Rumi. How unfair it seems, that after going through the trials and tribulations of life and finally gaining some wisdom, we have to die! And what will become of us after death? A Muslim is told about the wondrous gardens of paradise and the scorching fires of hell. Are these descriptions from the Qur'an to be taken literally or metaphorically? There is no definitive answer. We listen to a cacophony of voices from elders and authorities to glean insights, advice, and guidance, but the only certainty is that no one really knows.

The Purpose of Life

Even though we know very little about the mystery of life and death, people from all cultures and religions, all through the centuries, have persisted with one primary question: "What is the purpose of our existence?" Surely, our lives must have some meaning.

According to Islamic tradition, the Prophet Muhammad told his followers that the prophet David had pondered this very question and implored God for an answer. From the depths of Mystery, an answer arrived: "I was a secret Treasure and I longed to be known and so I created the worlds visible and invisible."[2] The purpose of life is encoded in those words and confirmed by verses of the Qur'an. God created the Heavens and the Earth not for "idle sport" but for "just ends" and a determined hour when all will be manifest. Through the words of the Qur'an, God tells us, "I have not created the invisible beings and men to any end other than that they may [know and] worship Me" (51:56). Fittingly, therefore, the Holy Book advises us in a later chapter, "Unto thy Sustainer turn with love" (94:8).

Spiritual teachers who have meditated on these verses tell us that we are placed on Earth to know God, and that to know God is to love the All-Merciful and Compassionate One. According to the Qur'an, Allah is *zahir* and *batin*, outside us and inside us. By doing the inner work of transforming our ego and opening our heart, we create pathways to connect with Divinity inside us. By serving humanity and God's creation, we connect to Divinity outside us. In other words, we have been placed on Earth for a dual mission: to evolve into the fullness of our being and to be of authentic service. By fulfilling our dual mission we get to know and love the Secret Treasure both within and without our own beings.

"Am I Not Your Sustainer?": Remembering the Covenant

Islamic sages teach that all human beings are cosmically encoded with a longing to connect with God. Occasionally, when we allow ourselves to think about it, we realize with Rumi that "this drunkenness must have started in some other tavern." An astonishing verse in the Qur'an (7:172) reveals that God gathered all the souls of unborn humanity before sending us to Earth, and spoke to us in the form of a question: "Am I not your Sustainer?—*Alastu bi Rabbikum?*" Thrilled to be hearing God's voice, in unison our souls joyously exclaimed, "Yes, yes, we testify!" This cosmic event constitutes the primordial covenant between God and humanity. But even though the covenant is seared into our souls, our memory of it is faded and muted once we arrive on Earth. Strangely, this forgetfulness is part of a divine design. Life is about the remembrance and realization of this original melody of *Alastu bi Rabbikum.*

Remembrance of our covenant does not come easily. We get so caught up in the loud doings of everyday life that we ignore the quieter urgings of our souls. Life events and experiences might jolt us into partial awakening, but we resist making changes to accommodate our spiritual longings because that can be very inconvenient. We humans don't lightly alter our lifestyles, aspirations, and priorities. That is truly a road less traveled. We avoid and deny, and soon we lapse into forgetfulness. We hide behind what Rumi calls the veils of health and wealth. When all is going well in our lives, we pay little attention to spiritual matters. When the veils are ripped by, say, a cancer diagnosis or a business failure, we may seek divine assistance, but when the crisis is over we quickly return to square one. The Qur'an knows this human tendency all too well: "And when a wave covers them like the canopy of clouds, they call to God, offering Him sincere devotion. But when He has delivered them safely to land, there are among them those who revert" (31:32).

A Mulla story builds on this verse and pokes fun at our human inclination to be unmindful of the Sustainer's role in our lives and to believe we can manage without divine support or intervention. The Mulla, as ferry captain, was privileged to have onboard some learned and wealthy dignitaries—scholars, lawyers, and businesspeople. To pass the time, they engaged the Mulla in conversation and goaded him to talk about his favorite topics. With growing amusement they watched the Mulla become animated as he talked about God, invisible realms, and the need to build faith in God. Some in the group chuckled softly.

Suddenly, a storm arose and grew fiercer by the moment. The ferryboat began to toss and turn helplessly. Fearful that all was lost, many of those people of reason got down on their knees and pleaded with God to save their lives. Promise after promise was offered—the kind we all make when we're desperate. The Mulla, calm and poised, walked among them and advised, "Friends! Friends! Steady now! Steady! Don't be so reckless with your goods." To the lawyers, he said, "Come on, drive a harder bargain!" To the businesspeople, "Hey! What about the bottom line?!" To the scholars, he chided, "Really now, first do more research before making wild promises." To all of them he exclaimed tongue-in-cheek, "By all means, avoid entanglements in your life just as you have so far."

Peering into the distance, suddenly the Mulla shouted in excitement, "Ahoy! Ahoy! I see land!" And the story concludes just as one might expect: The passengers stood up, dusted off their knees, and celebrated with hardly a thought about their desperately promised "entanglements."

Tauba: Turning to God

However busily we may seek to avoid it, sooner or later we will connect with this innate inner longing to bond with something greater than our human ego. It cannot be otherwise. "There is some kiss we want with our whole lives," says Rumi; we ache for "the touch of

Spirit on the body." One way or another, the circumstances of our lives will awaken a vague memory of our primordial covenant and we will begin the search for connection with the Secret Treasure. This awakening is called *tauba*, which means a "turning to God." Our souls rejoice exuberantly because we have made the turn, and the joy turns us into genuine seekers. We have finally come out of our slumber and are willing to be vulnerable. We make commitments in our own way to strive to become better persons and to be of service to others. We might experience difficulties and doubts on the road ahead, but there is no turning back. Once the blush of the Beloved graces you, say the Sufis, there is no going back to being a green apple.

This illuminative moment of *tauba* suffuses a person in a variety of ways. It could arise from a series of life events or seemingly from a single incident. Sometimes it is in the awareness of death that the moment of turning arrives in its fullest glory.

Deborah, to give one example, is a corporate executive who had no use for religion or spirituality. A variety of life crises would bring her closer to God for a while, but then she would back away because of her distaste for organized religion. The turning point for her started with an utterly devastating divorce followed by three years of unremitting sadness. Nothing in her material world brought her comfort and consolation: not therapy, not cruises, not Internet dating. Her heart, she felt, was irreparably broken and she didn't know where to turn. All that changed in a heartbeat when she read a few lines by the fourteenth-century Sufi poet Hafiz. As achingly rendered by Daniel Ladinsky in his book *The Subject Tonight Is Love*, Hafiz cries out:

> *Something missing in my heart tonight*
> *Has made my eyes so soft,*
> *My voice so tender*
> *My need for God absolutely clear.*

Today, Deborah has an active spiritual life and feels that her inner work has made her a more authentic human being. Describing herself as "spiritual but not religious," she is on the journey from personality to real persona, or her authentic being. Echoing the language and sentiment of the Sufi poets she loves so much, she now says that the soil of her being was roughly turned over by her divorce, which made it ready to receive the "God seed." By grace of God and her own hard work, that seed took root, sprouted, and is in full bloom.

Adnan Mahmud is a fine example of *tauba* inspired by a single incident. As a young man, Adnan came from Bangladesh to study in America and, by dint of hard work and sacrifice, he secured a lucrative position with Microsoft in Seattle. He climbed the ladder of success but felt a yearning for something that neither money nor power could satisfy. Then one day, while visiting Bangladesh on business, he came across a poor and grief-stricken father who was carrying the dead body of his son aimlessly in the streets. Adnan instinctively wanted to help, but he had appointments to keep so, reluctantly, he traveled on. But the encounter weighed on him and pierced his heart. Something opened up in him and he felt a shift, a turning in a different direction. In a sudden burst of awakening, he realized that he had been climbing the wrong ladder. Today, he continues to work at Microsoft, but his motivation is to earn money to fund a nonprofit foundation called Jolkona, which he and his wife established to help the poor and marginalized. Along with his work to serve Allah *zahir* (Divinity manifested in others), Adnan performs spiritual practices to maintain connection with Allah *batin* (the Divinity at the core of his being).

And finally, my friend Abdi Sami epitomizes *tauba* occasioned by awareness of death. Abdi's fifty-five-year-old body is riddled with cancerous tumors and he knows his days are numbered. In his intense grieving process after he got the diagnosis, he was startled one day to hear the familiar Islamic call to prayer being sung in an exquisitely beautiful tone and melody. This was all the more surprising because, although he had been born a Muslim, he had turned away from Islam early in life, owing to disillusionment with the hypocrisy of the mullahs and their institutions. But here was this beautiful summons to prayer, which was clearly an internal sound, because it was completely inaudible to the people around him. Something shifted, and Abdi was aware of what he calls the "Beloved" in his heart. Since that time, he has often heard the internal call, and when it happens, all the ego-driven *I* and *me* impulses simply dissolve. He feels, for a few precious moments, an inexpressible connection with the Beloved within him. The most astounding discovery for him is the realization that there is unbounded love in the depths of his being. This discovery brings him to tears whenever he talks about it. Now his greatest aspiration is to share this unbounded love with everyone around him. This is his primary motivation to linger longer on Earth. At the time of this writing, Abdi has miraculously exceeded all time lines of longevity gingerly set by his doctors, and his spirit is radiant with joy and aliveness. When asked how he can be so radiant in the face of death, Abdi replies with a favorite verse from the Qur'an:

> *Say: "Truly, my prayer*
> *And my service of sacrifice,*
> *My life and my death,*
> *Are [all] for Allah,*
> *The Cherisher of the Worlds."*

(6:162)

REFLECTIONS
AND
PRACTICE

+ In "The Speed of Darkness," the poet Muriel Rukeyser wrote, "The Universe is made of stories, not of atoms." What is your story of a *tauba* moment or moments that awakened a longing in you and made you turn in the direction of Spirit? Reflect on your story and be present with any feelings that surface in you. These are sacred moments that beg to be cherished and honored. Remembrances and reflections will open up something beautiful in you.

✦ The rigors of the spiritual journey can bring periods of sadness and depression. There is sacredness in these times of burden and confusion. Can you create or join a circle of friends who can offer you support? How can you be gentle with yourself?

"We Have Not Known You as We Should Have"

(HADITH)

TOWARD THE END OF HIS LIFE, THE PROPHET MUHAMMAD humbly lamented: "O Allah, we have not known you as we should have." Even for the Prophet, it was not humanly possible to know all that he might have wanted to know about his Creator. Allah, as God is called in Arabic, is Absolute Mystery. God is beyond space, time, gender, and form. In a hadith, God says, "I am as my servant thinks I am," and the Qur'an states, "Every moment He manifests Himself in another glorious state" (55:29). The seventeenth-century spiritual adept Dara Shikoh began his poetry with the invocation, "In the name of Him Who has no name, Who appears by whichever name you will call Him."[1]

So far beyond the comprehension of even the most enlightened human mind is the eternal splendor of our Creator that we cannot begin to fathom or describe it. Our poor efforts are like using a bamboo stick to measure the depth of the ocean. Or, as the Qur'an reveals:

And even if all the trees on Earth were pens,
And the oceans ink, backed by seven more oceans,

The words of God would not be exhausted:
For God is infinite in power and wisdom.

(31:27)

God Is Compassion: But What of Suffering?

With our limited human faculties we can never know God directly, but we can begin to experience our Creator indirectly—to feel what mystics describe as the "glow of Presence"—by reflecting on the ninety-nine divine attributes or "beautiful names" mentioned in the Islamic tradition. Of these, the one most frequently mentioned is *compassion,* a word that connotes deep caring, empathy, sympathy, and willingness to forgive. Indeed, the Qur'an opens with a paean to the God of compassion—"Cherisher and Sustainer of the Worlds, Most Gracious, Most Merciful" (1:2–3)—and virtually every chapter begins with the words, "In the name of God, Boundlessly Merciful and Compassionate." Throughout the Qur'an, verses remind us of the many aspects of divine compassion. Our Guardian-Lord (2:21) shelters orphans (93:6), guides the wanderer (93:7), grants ample forgiveness (53:32), and, in words attributed to the prophet Moses, is "the Most Merciful of those who show mercy" (7:151). This is but a tiny sampling of Qur'anic verses extolling compassion as the very essence of God. "Call upon God, or call upon the Merciful; by whatever name ye call upon Him, it is well" (17:110).

The skeptics among us may say, "These are lovely sentiments, but are they really true?" Divine compassion is not much in evidence when we look at the world around us. Human history is filled with a plethora of plagues, earthquakes, tidal waves, killings, injustice, oppression, suffering, and pain. Would a compassionate God allow these terrible afflictions? It cannot be that God is not aware: "He knoweth whatever there is on the Earth and in the sea. Not a leaf doth fall but with His knowledge" (6:59). It cannot be that God lacks power: "When He hath decreed a Plan, He but saith to it, 'Be,' and it is!" (3:47). How could an all-compassionate, all-knowing, and all-powerful God allow such pain and tragedy to occur in the world that He truly sustains and cherishes?

There is no humanly satisfactory and logical answer to this question. Some Sufi teachers say they desist from asking such questions, lest God should turn the questions back on them. Perhaps they are mindful of the legend about the holy man who traveled the world, seeing all the pain and suffering that people must endure. "Allah!" he cried. "Why don't you do something about it?" "Ah, but I did," came the gentle response: "I created *you*." Aside from our personal efforts to heal the world (Jewish readers will recognize this as *tikkun olam*, repairing the world), all we can do is contemplate the words of the prophet Job in the darkest hour of his suffering: "Truly distress has seized me, but Thou art the Most Merciful of those that are Merciful" (21:83).

As a counselor I have sat with people who felt so brutalized by life and betrayed by God that they specifically requested that I not mention God in the healing sessions. One was beside herself with grief because her daughter had been murdered, one had suffered incest by a cruel and dominating father, and one was haunted by the death of his father, a revolutionary who had been thrown off a helicopter by government forces. I meticulously avoided any reference to God, but amazingly, in the process of their healing all three people of their own accord brought God into their lives and developed an unshakable faith in Divinity. In fact, they have become such ardent and passionate devotees that I am reminded of a tongue-in-cheek Sufi song from South Asia: "O God, save me from all these God lovers!" This phenomenon is consistent with a traditional story about a penniless Bedouin who was asked if he believed in the all-compassionate God. Replied the simple man, "You mean the God who has sent me poverty, illnesses, afflictions, and has made me naked and sent me wandering from country to country?" But as he spoke, he entered into a state of ecstasy. This Bedouin was obviously a soul mate of the prophet Job.

A Greater Mystery

The paradoxes of God are evident in the heartfelt declarations of Sufi seekers who, after years of inner work and service, come to the amazing realization that God is the seeker and we are the ones being sought. Pointing to verses in the Qur'an that ask us humans to "help God" (47:7) or "loan to God a goodly loan" (57:11), the mystics are astounded that we who owe everything we are to God should be asked the favor of a loan back to God. Rumi tenderly muses that the Holy One suffers His absence in us and cries out to Himself. The holiest of mysteries, he says, is that our relationship with God is intimate beyond belief. Not only do the thirsty seek water but Water seeks the thirsty. This is not about God being needy but about an infinite tenderness and graciousness, about the divine longing to be known and loved by us mere mortals. Such a mystery is beyond human comprehension. As the Creator tells us in the Qur'an, "Of knowledge We have given you but a little" (17:85).

Beyond Form to Essence

Sadly, our lack of definitive knowledge about Divinity does not prevent us from arguing, fighting, and even killing over our definitions of God. The human ego is fiercely attached to its minuscule understanding of God. A companion of the Prophet once asked him if he had seen his Sustainer. The Prophet replied, "He is Light. Where shall I see Him?" Spiritual teachers use the metaphor of light to illustrate our attachment to form. Sunlight falls on this wall, on that wall, and on yet another, producing a different play of light and shadow on each wall. Each wall receives a "borrowed splendor." And here is the question posed by spiritual adepts: "Why do you set your heart on a piece of brick?" Seek the Source of Light that shines forever. Our descriptions of God are different, but sages in every tradition have intuited that the Source is One. We are asked to go beyond form and enter into essence.

Decades ago in the village of Mahdipur in Bangladesh, my grandfather would admonish Muslim villagers who criticized their

Hindu neighbors for practicing idolatry. He had an appreciative understanding of Hinduism and patiently explained that the gods and goddesses represent different facets of Divinity and they all point to the One Supreme Being, called Brahma in Hinduism. True idolatry, he explained, is about worshiping the false gods of the ego, such as money and power. Grandfather loved the Hindu definition of God: "The eyes cannot see It but It is that by which the eyes see; the ears cannot hear It but It is that by which the ears hear.... the tongue cannot utter It but It is that by which the tongue utters; the mind cannot think It but It is that by which the mind thinks." To my grandfather, this was just another way of expressing a favorite hadith qudsi in which God says of His faithful servant: "I am his hearing with which he hears, his sight with which he sees, his hand with which he grasps, and his foot with which he walks."

One of my father's best friends was Mr. Sunthorn, a Thai diplomat who was often posted to the same countries as my father. Our families spent many hours together and enjoyed learning about the similarities and differences between our religions—Islam and Buddhism. These discussions were often graced by Buddhist and Muslim teachers, so the level of exchange was quite scholarly and creditable. It became astonishingly clear that the Buddhist concept of Nirvana is akin to the monotheistic understanding of Godhead. Nirvana is described as unborn, eternal, uncompounded, unmitigated, and filled with abiding joy. My father and the Muslim scholars often joked that the devout Buddhist, Mr. Sunthorn, was one of the best Muslims they knew!

In Essence God Is One

Some revelations in the Qur'an strongly criticize the Christian belief that Jesus is the incarnate Son of God. A brief chapter memorized by countless Muslim children emphasizes that God "neither begets nor is begotten" (112:3). God is "the One and Only," says the Holy Book, and "there is none like unto Him" (112:4). Although the Qur'an may criticize a Christian belief, it does not condemn Christian believers. In fact, one verse says that "nearest in love to [Muslims] are those who say 'We are Christians'" (5:82), especially those who are devoted to learning and are not arrogant. Though the Qur'an makes harsh statements about some Jews for not living up to their covenant with God, it does not condemn their beliefs. In fact, Muslims and Jews share a remarkably similar belief in one God. The Holy Book makes it clear that beyond the forms of belief, the Source is One. The Qur'an instructs Muslims to say to both Jews and Christians, "We believe in the Revelation that has come down to us and in that which came down to you; our God and your God is One" (29:46).

Differences in the details of our various beliefs need not be a source of conflict. In fact, the Holy Book suggests that religious diversity is intentionally designed by God to be a blessing. "To every people was sent an Apostle" (10:47), says the Qur'an, and "Verily, those who have attained to faith [in this divine writ], as well as those who follow the Jewish faith, and the Christians and the Sabians [Islamic scholars conjecture that Sabians might refer to the followers of John the Baptist, or Zoroastrians, or a community associated with the Queen of Sheba]—all who believe in God and the Last Day and do righteous deeds—shall have their reward with their Sustainer; and no fear need they have, and neither shall they grieve" (2:62). In my interfaith congregation, a number of atheists and agnostics worship alongside Muslims and non-Muslims. I tell them sincerely that, in my understanding, they do believe in God. They simply call God by a different name: Truth, Humanity, Compassion, Justice—whatever stirs their heart and motivates them to work for good is truly divine.

Stages of Knowledge about God

Ultimately, our knowledge of God is a personal experience. All the theologies of the world are as nothing compared with what the mystics describe as a "whisper of the Beloved" or the "glow of Presence."

Belief based on what our teachers call "borrowed certainty" is no substitute for an inner experience of Divinity.

According to the Qur'an, we progress in faith from simple belief to inner certainty in three stages (102:5, 102:7, 69:51). In the first stage, called *ilm ul yaqin* ("the knowledge of belief"), our faith is based on hearsay. This is a necessary stage and a good starting point, but there is danger if we get stuck here. The temptation is strong to become loud and self-righteous. Thus we need to move to the next stage, called *ayn ul yaqin* ("the eye of belief"), that is, belief based on personal witness. The signs of God are everywhere "in the utmost horizons [of the universe] and within themselves" (41:53) and we are asked to be present and open to experiences that expand our minds and open our hearts. Repeatedly the Qur'an asks, "Will you not see?" and "Will you not understand?" We are asked to acquire our own experience of the signs of God. This deepens faith. In the final stage, *haq ul yaqin* ("the total reality of belief"), our belief emerges from an experience of inner truth. This stage is fulfilled when we are doing our inner work and acquire a unique personal knowing of Mystery. The Sufis put it succinctly: "Those who taste, know." At this stage, we become gentle and quiet with our knowing. We feel graced by the glow of Presence. There is no need to say or do, but simply to be. Rumi says that we are content to simply chew quietly on our sugarcane love of God.

Sufis elaborate on the three stages with a metaphorical story of a moth that first hears of the beauty of the flame of a candle, then actually witnesses it, and finally hurls itself into the flame. In the last stage, it dies to conjectures and theories about the flame, and comes alive with experience of an inner truth.

In a hadith, God says tenderly to humanity, "Between Me and you there are no veils but between you and Me there are seventy thousand veils."[2] Our souls yearn to know and love God. Sooner or later we shall turn in that direction and begin to remove the veils little by little and with compassion for ourselves. This is the inner work we are called to do on Earth, without which it is not possible to know God or feel fulfilled in life.

REFLECTIONS

- ✦ Ask yourself, "What is my image of God? What does it mean that God is both inside and outside of me? How does this dovetail with our understanding of God as genderless, formless, and omnipresent?"
- ✦ What experiences in your life have brought you closer to God? What events have separated you from God? What sustains your faith in God?

PRACTICE

Sufis say that the following practice, done regularly, "opens doors" between human heart and divine Heart. The Qur'an says that when we experience this connection with Divinity, our skins and hearts "soften to the celebration of God's praises" (39:23).

Getting to know God can be as simple as knowing your own breath. In fact, the Sufis say that God is the Breath within the breath.

- ✦ Close your eyes, focus on your nostrils, and gently be present with your breath. If thoughts or images intervene and you become distracted, be compassionate with yourself. Simply bring your attention back to your nostrils and continue being mindful of your breath.

✦ Now, with each inhalation, intone silently "Allah" and with each exhalation, silently repeat "Allah."

✦ An alternative verse is "*La ila ha il Allah*—There is no God but God." Traditionally, this breath meditation starts with an exhalation. With the outbreath, invoke the words "*La ila ha*"; breathing in, say, "*il Allah*."

CULTIVATING INNER SPACIOUSNESS

"Know Thyself and You Shall Know Thy Lord"

(HADITH)

OUR FRIEND THE MULLA TRAVELS TO CHINA AND ENTERS a bank for a financial transaction. When the bank official asks him to verify his identity, the Mulla reaches into his pocket and pulls out a pocket mirror. Peering into the mirror for some time, the Mulla finally declares, "Yep! That's me all right! I do certify it!"

Muslims will recognize the Mulla's journey to China as a reference to an oft-quoted but unauthenticated hadith: "To seek knowledge, travel as far as China." Both the Qur'an and related teachings urge us to go to great lengths to acquire knowledge. The story also points to the critical need for *self*-knowledge. Getting to know ourselves is a sacred undertaking for, as the Prophet Muhammad declared, "Know thyself and you shall know thy Lord."[1] Without self-knowledge, we shall never know the spark of Divinity within us. Spiritual teachers urge us to move from the personality masks that we wear in this world to our real face. Our authentic face is the most beautiful.

The advice is simple, but the task is not easy. Sadly, we are conditioned to define ourselves and others by superficial realities. We focus on what we have and what we do, rather than on being and expressing our most authentic, essential selves. We identify ourselves and one another on the basis of education, profession, family, or financial status, and we miss out on the inner reality. This has sorry consequences for the choices we make and the way we experience our lives. If we have no connection to our divine essence, living only to satisfy the needs and desires of the ego-driven personality, we are indeed living what Henry David Thoreau famously called "lives of quiet desperation." In the too-few years between what seems to be a meaningless birth and what we fear is the nonbeing of death, we grasp at whatever pleasures and material benefits life has to offer, never fully satisfied and always looking for more. Such a life is but a dim shadow of what our Creator and Cherisher has in mind for us.

The sacred work of getting to know ourselves gradually diminishes the shadow and brings us closer to the Light. Little by little, with each level of higher awareness we remove the veils that separate us from the Light. We become aware of some astonishing truths about ourselves that are confirmed by verses in the Qur'an.

Ruby in the Midst of Granite

The Holy Book says that God lovingly molded us from water and clay and then infused us with divine breath (15:29, 38:72). Is it not astonishing to realize that each of us carries that spark of Divinity?! So precious and unique are we humans that God commanded the angels to bow in obeisance to the beauty of our divine essence. Sufi poets and teachers expound on the astounding possibilities that we humans possess. Rumi cries out to us, "You are a ruby in the midst of granite! How long will you continue to deceive us?" Begging us to do the inner work so that we can return to the "root of the root" of our real self, he tells us that he knows about our sacred essence, for "we can see the look in your eyes."

The ninth-century teacher Bayazid Bistami persisted with his inner work and was dazzled by the blaze of consciousness that overcame him. "Glory be to me!" he exclaimed. "How great is my majesty!"[2]

Earlier in the century the Sufi teacher Al Hallaj burst out, "I am the Truth" and said in bewilderment, "I went from God to God, until He cried from me in me, 'O Thou I!'"[3] These beatific expressions, not of ego but of sheer enlightenment, echo the Prophet Muhammad's exquisite exclamation when, in a moment of epiphany, he declared, "I am He and He is I except that I am I and He is He!"[4]

One could reasonably object that such extraordinary revelations may be possible for sages, but not for us ordinary mortals. But Rumi, that champion of our ruby essence, insists that it is indeed possible for any of us to bond with our higher self. As proof, he cites the example of his own life. He was the intellectual type, a scholar overly engrossed in mental activities, until he met his teacher, Shams of Tabriz. Once he accepted Shams's challenge to focus on his inner work, his heart opened to a world of ecstatic joy and he was graced with sublime poetry that seemed to pour from the invisible realms. His body was truly the Spirit's dwelling place, and his lips declared the holy mysteries. Even if we ordinary seekers do not channel divine poetry, don't we occasionally glimpse, connect with, and rhapsodize over fragments of our innate nobility, exquisite graciousness, and heart-melting kindness? Don't we sometimes ache to do some abiding good in this world so that we can make a difference? According to Rumi, it is the silent, mysterious vibration of God's breath within us yearning for us to awaken. Spirit within us, breaking through layers of our ego, screams out, "Enough is enough! How long can the Ocean abide in a water skin!"

The Slinking Whisperer

What mutes this divine voice and causes confusion is another voice that asserted itself during that moment of cosmic creation mentioned earlier, when our Creator commanded the angels to bow down to our sacred essence (15:29 and 38:72). The angels did prostrate themselves, says the Qur'an, but "not so *Iblis*: He refused to be among those who prostrated themselves" (15:30; 38:74). Arguing with God, the haughty *Iblis*—often called Satan (*Shaitan* in Arabic) and also known among Muslims as "the slinking whisperer"—declared that he would do his best to "make wrong fair-seeming to them on Earth" (15:39) and "put them all in the wrong" (38:82). Of course, the all-powerful God could have dismissed *Iblis* and his schemes in an instant, but Islamic teaching holds that, instead, our Creator allows the slinking whisperer to waylay us in order to help us build our spiritual muscles. It is a Qur'anic principle that "Of everything We have created pairs [or opposites] that ye may receive instruction" (51:49), and this includes the lower and higher selves of the human psyche. "We created the being in the highest station, then brought him down, lowest of the low, except those who keep the faith, and work justice, theirs is a recompense unending" (95:4–6). Thus at every moment we have choices to make. Whose inner voice shall we listen to—the voice of our divine essence or the whispering voice that seduces us into following the instincts of the untamed ego?

The Qur'an identifies three stages of the ego and says that the primary purpose of our lives is to work through these stages to a point of complete surrender of our ego to God. It involves the deep alignment of our ego-driven personality with the sacred essence at the core of our being. In this state, the soul can truly cry, "O Thou I!"

To know ourselves is to be mindful of the voices, vibrations, impulses, and inclinations that draw us closer to or further from our true Selves. It is to become aware of the conditioning that has led us into harmful behavioral patterns, such as self-righteousness, pettiness, aggression, dishonesty, and blaming others for our misdeeds, and to rewrite our inner tapes so that we become more tolerant, generous, gentle, honest, and responsible for our own choices. This is not an easy task. Such are the beguiling and subtle tendencies of the ego to be self-righteous that even enlightened beings suffer lapses and have to work continually to be aware and vigilant.

Even prophets have to struggle with the nature of being human. In a chapter called *Abasa,* which means "He frowned," the Qur'an talks about a time when the Prophet was engaged in conversation about Islam with an arrogant tribal chieftain, but was interrupted by a question from a blind old man who had been listening. Feeling impatient because he was interrupted, the Prophet frowned. Later the Prophet had a revelation. "As to one who regards himself as self-sufficient, to him you pay attention ... but as for the one who came eagerly to you and with an inner awe, him you disregarded. By no means should this be so" (80:5–10).

These and countless other stories and confessions from all spiritual traditions demonstrate that even prophets have to struggle with the nature of being human. According to Muhammad, only two humans were ever spared the difficulty of dealing with the slinking whisperer: Jesus and his mother, Mary. When asked if he too had a slinking whisperer, the Prophet said, "Yes, but don't be alarmed, for I have made him a Muslim!"—meaning not that his personal demon was a member of the Muslim faith, but that it was on the path of surrender to God.

Patterns and Direction

Two Islamic teaching stories come to mind whenever I think about my own patterns of behavior. The first pokes gentle fun at the human tendency to get stuck in a rut and stay there, unconscious that the rut is of our own making. The Mulla opens his brown bag every day at lunchtime, discovers yet another cheese sandwich, and complains that he is getting sick and tired of those lousy sandwiches. Finally his coworkers suggest that maybe he should persuade his wife to pack a different kind of lunch. "But I'm not married," says the Mulla. "Well, then, who makes your lunch every day?" they ask. "I do!" says the Mulla.

In the second story, which reminds me to look inward for solutions to what may be troubling me, the ninth-century sage Rabia was looking for a lost key under a streetlight. Her neighbors turned out to help, but without success. Finally, they asked where she might have dropped the key, so that they could better focus their search. "Actually," said Rabia, "I lost it in my house." Bemused, they asked her why she didn't look for it there. "Because," she said, "there's no light in my house, but out here the light is bright!" The neighbors laughed, and Rabia seized the moment to make her point. "Friends," she said, "you are intelligent people and that is why you laugh. But tell me: When you lose your joy or peace of mind because of some disappointment or hardship, did you lose it out there [gesturing around her] or in here [gesturing to her heart]?" We tend to lay blame on our external circumstances and seek superficial solutions, but the truth is that we lost our peace and joy inside ourselves. We avoid looking inside us, where the light is dim.

When we make it a lifelong practice to shine the light of compassionate awareness on ourself, our shadow gently begins to diminish, and we come closer to discovering our radiant, divine Self.

REFLECTIONS

Can you identify at least one "cheese sandwich" pattern of behavior you are stuck in?

Are you mindful of at least two negative traits in yourself that you would like to diminish, and two beautiful qualities that reflect your authentic self and that you want to expand?

PRACTICE

The Qur'an says, "There is a watcher within, ever present" (50:18). You can activate a connection with this sacred light of self-witnessing.

Gently touch your heart and make a prayerful intention to continuously be aware of your heart. If your attention strays, touch your heart again to remind yourself. This repeated focus on the heart activates a mysterious light of compassionate self-witnessing.

"Die Before You Die"

(HADITH)

ONCE WE TRULY BEGIN THE WORK OF GETTING TO know ourselves, we come face-to-face with our untamed ego, which is going to struggle mightily to maintain pride of place in our internal makeup. Speaking of this struggle between the ego and the higher self, the Prophet Muhammad said to his followers, "Die before you die."[1] By this he meant not that we must kill the ego, but that in the course of our life—that is, before we die a physical death—we must learn to let go of our attachment to the ego. This is not to condemn the ego, for it is an integral and divinely created part of our being that enables us to function in the world. Indeed, we cannot "kill" or abolish our God-given ego, but we can and must work to transform it so that it collaborates and aligns with our higher self.

Islamic spirituality abounds with metaphors for the peaceful merging of the lower and higher self. Rumi observes that we need a candle flame to find our way in the dark, but once we venture into the land of the Radiant Sun, the flame of the candle is subsumed in the glory of the Sun's illumination. The candle flame may seem to be annihilated, but it is still alive: Place a cloth to it and it will catch fire.

Three Stages of Ego

To usher in our inner light, we are asked to transform the three stages of the ego, called *nafs* in the Qur'an. In the first stage, *nafs al-amma-rah* (headstrong ego), we are manipulated by an ego that is a "commanding master" and sometimes inclines us toward wrongdoing (12:53). In this stage, the ego wants to dominate and feel superior and may even violate ethical standards to maintain its superiority. With compassion, effort, and vigilance, we can transform the commanding master into a personal assistant.

In the second stage, *nafs al-lawwama* (self-reproaching ego), we become aware of the voice of conscience and learn to make right choices (75:2). If we are persistent in resisting the unworthy urgings of the commanding master and reinforce our efforts with spiritual practices, we will transform the competitive ego into a collaborative ego.

In the last stage, *nafs al-mutma'inna* (ego at peace), the ego is aligned with our sacred essence and is no longer struggling for ascendance. In Islamic parlance it is said that we have surrendered our ego to the will of God, and in return we experience what the Qur'an calls *Sakinah,* or inner peace (89:27). Life still has its trials and tribulations, but they no longer cause chronic distress. We become like the Buddhist monk whose house accidentally burned to the ground one moonlit night. Saddened but not dismayed, the monk gazed at the moon and remarked with equanimity, "Ah, finally, a perfect view of the moon at night!"

The Greater *Jihad:* The Spiritual Work of Opening the Heart

Transformation of the ego is the work of a lifetime—a lifetime lived one day at a time, with renewed intention and vigilant effort each day. The Mulla knew this when he teased the townspeople by mounting the public dais and asking, "Do you want to know the secret to obtaining salvation without effort, freedom without sacrifice, riches without work, and knowledge without study?" Oh, yes, they wanted that secret, and he promised to tell them in good time. He repeated the offer on several occasions, and each time the crowd grew larger and clamored more loudly to know the secret. "All in good time," he told them, and the story goes on to say that he became a wealthy man by preaching about expensive secret formulas and clever schemes.

The real secret is that without effort the ego does not give in easily. The struggle is ongoing, but the rewards are worth the cost. Numerous revelations in the Qur'an address the need for constant exertion to manifest our higher selves. "The human being can have nothing but that for which he strives" (53:39), and "Verily never will Allah change the condition of a people until they change what is within themselves" (13:11). The word *jihad* is a discomfiting word unless we know its true meaning. *Jihad* literally means "effort" or "exertion."

Effort and exertion are needed in countless fields of human endeavor. As individuals, we expend a great deal of effort to succeed in our studies, our jobs, our relationships. As communities, we strive for good schools, secure food sources, adequate health care, and safe neighborhoods. On a larger scale, we try to help those in our own country or abroad who have been struck by disastrous earthquakes and tsunamis. And, yes, sometimes we even go to war in defense of what we think is right. All these efforts fall under the banner of *jihad*, but some kinds of *jihad* are greater than others.

Sadly, most non-Muslims associate *jihad* with war and violence because of the criminal acts of terrorists who misinterpret Qur'anic verses. In the context of prolonged warfare on the Arabian Peninsula during the seventh century, the Qur'an permitted Muslims to defend themselves from attack, but it warned them, "Begin not hostilities for God loves not the aggressors" (2:190). If, during battle, the attacker sued for peace, Muslims were commanded to lay down their arms, because "God loves those who restrain themselves" (2:194). As things developed, the Prophet Muhammad and his embryonic community did have to defend themselves against attacks from the Quraish tribe and its allies, who were overwhelmingly superior in number and arms. On one occasion after returning from a battle, the Prophet said, "You have returned from the lesser *jihad* to the greater *jihad*." In surprise they asked, "What is the greater *jihad*?" The Prophet replied, "The greater *jihad* is the struggle with one's own ego."[2]

So the greater *jihad* is the spiritual work of transforming the ego and opening the heart, and that is the primary focus of this book. It also refers to the efforts we must make to improve our relationships with family and friends, as well as the exertions we undertake to foster justice and care for God's creation. The lesser *jihad* is about defending oneself when attacked. But even a "just war" is inherently dehumanizing, and we know from the daily news the depths to which the untamed ego can sink in the heat of battle. It is far easier to de-humanize the other and seek revenge than to see the divine in our enemies and strive for peace with them.

Birth Pangs

As mentioned earlier, Jesus and his mother, Mary, are the only two humans who have lived without being troubled by the "slinking whisperer." Jesus is revered in Islam as a prophet "held in honor in this world and the hereafter and of the company of those nearest to God" (3:45), and Mary is similarly admired as the woman chosen by God "above the women of all nations" (3:42). But even these extraordinary beings had their share of struggles, beginning with Mary's difficult labor at Jesus's birth. The Qur'an tells us that the pain "… drove her to the trunk of a palm tree: She cried in her anguish: 'Ah! Would that I had died before this!'" (19:23). But a voice cried to her from beneath the tree, "Grieve not! For thy Lord hath provided a rivulet beneath thee; and shake toward thyself the trunk of the palm tree: It will let fall fresh ripe dates upon thee. So eat and drink and cool thine eyes" (19:24–6). This story, so touchingly human in its details, assures us that as we labor to bring forth our higher self (what Islamic spirituality actually refers to as our "inner Jesus"), our compassionate

Sustainer will grace us with the spiritual equivalent of fresh dates and cool water for our weeping eyes. "With every difficulty there is relief," says the Qur'an (94:5), and it repeats as if it knows we need reassurance: "Verily, with every difficulty there is relief" (94:6).

REFLECTIONS AND PRACTICE

✦ Prophet Muhammad's challenge to "Die before you die" means that we have to do the inner work of dying to all that is false in us so that we can give birth to our divine essence. This is the way to fully experience joy, peace, intimacy, and fulfillment. What are the falsehoods in your life that you need to die to?

✦ Rumi reminds us of the existential importance of this task. He tells us that we might know the value of every item of merchandise, "but if you don't know the value of your own soul, it's all foolishness." What are the personal qualities that you most value in yourself? In others?

✦ The work is hard, but the rewards are real. A hadith qudsi says, "When my servant draws near to Me a handbreadth, I draw near to him an arm's length; if he draws near to me an arm's length, I draw near to him a fathom; if he approaches me walking, I approach him running." Have you ever experienced help, guidance, or a sign from the invisible world in a palpable way? What happened? What was the situation? How did this impact you?

GEM 7

"The Road Is Long, the Sea Is Deep"

(FARIDUDDIN ATTAR)

IN SUFI LITERATURE, THE TWELFTH-CENTURY ALLEGORI-
cal poem of approximately 4,500 words, called "Conference of the
Birds," by the spiritual teacher Fariduddin Attar is a celebrated classic. Many students of Islamic spirituality pore over the nuances of
this tale.

Attar's story of the birds—full of humor, pathos, and mystical
experiences—is the story of our lifelong journey toward union with
our divine Source.

In brief, the birds of the world gather at a convention and talk
about their discontented lives. Even though this world offers moments of happiness, deep inside they feel a strange ache and dissatisfaction, which boils down to the desire for a "king," someone greater
than their avian selves. The hoopoe bird, who has traveled far and
wide and knows the ways of the invisible world, tells them that they
already have such a king, the Simorgh, who is as close to them as they
are far from him. Proof of the Simorgh's existence has been found in
China, he says—yet another reference to the Prophet's injunction to
travel as far as China in search of truth.

To the birds' utter delight, the hoopoe knows how to reach the Simorgh and offers to be their guide. It won't be easy, he warns: "The road is long, the sea is deep."[1]

At first, throwing caution to the winds, the birds are seized with an intense longing to fly to the Simorgh right away. But then they begin to reconsider. "One must have the heart of a lion," the hoopoe has said—but they are only birds. Moreover, the hoopoe explains that the path traverses seven arduous valleys: that of the Quest, Love, Understanding, Detachment, Unity, Bewilderment, and, finally, Death. And in each valley, a hundred difficulties and trials will assail the seeker. And so their resolve begins to weaken. One by one they make their excuses, each representing a human fault that prevents us from doing the inner work to attain enlightenment.

With emotion and passion, the nightingale declares that he is so deeply in love with the rose that he cannot even think about his own existence. It is for him that the rose flowers with a hundred petals. What more could he wish for? The hoopoe chides the nightingale for being so dazzled by the exterior form of things and advises him to forsake the rose and blush for himself. Is he not aware that the rose's smile fades within a day? Why is the nightingale—why are we—so attached to our ephemeral delights?

The parrot, which has lived its life in a gilded cage, wants only to guard its security. "You are a cringing slave!" cries the hoopoe, but the parrot is too afraid to venture forth. It is the same with the glittering peacock, strutting with pride and afraid to risk his plumage. His colors are fashioned by the Painter of the world and he is destined to live in earthly paradise. The hoopoe berates him for not understanding that the paradise of earthly bliss is only a little drop in the vast ocean of the Most High.

Then comes the duck (already pure enough in his watery environment), the partridge (convinced that he needs no other goal in life than to pluck jewels from the Earth), the hawk (content to perch on the leather-clad wrist of his handler), the heron (the sea suffices for him), and the owl (his love is solely for gold's buried glory). Bringing up the rear is the finch, who pleads that her body is fragile and her feathers are too weak to carry her the distance to the Simorgh's sanctuary. A reasonable excuse, one might think, but the hoopoe is not moved by the finch's artful pleas. Whatever our perceived strengths or lack thereof, we are not excused from the journey. The finch's humility is a cover for a hundred signs of vanity and pride.

Having dispatched all manner of excuses, the hoopoe then encounters an unnamed bird who claims to be satisfied with his spiritual state just as it is. Squawking that he has achieved wise perfection through a life of self-denial, he demands to know why he should roam in deserts and mountains far from home. For him the hoopoe has the harshest words of all. If the self-satisfied bird does not free himself from constant thoughts of *me* and *I* and if any dominant thought or taste of self-centeredness lingers, he is damned in whatever he may do.

Many more birds come forward with excuses to which the hoopoe makes replies. Finally, the resolute ones among them embark on the journey.

The Spiritual Journey's Seven Valleys

The valleys of which the hoopoe speaks are the stages of the spiritual journey. First is the Valley of the Quest, in which one learns through much striving and grieving to let go of the nonessentials and begin to purify the heart for its sacred encounter. Next comes the Valley of Love, where we abandon our weak, backsliding ways and commit ourselves with a burning passion to our soul's true delight. In the Valley of Understanding, we learn to discern the spiritual path that works best for us. In the Valley of Detachment, we shed our need to be in "control" as we come to terms with life's realities, accepting whatever comes our way with grace and humility. Stripped of the illusion that we alone are the center of our little universe, we fly on to the Valley of Unity. Here we realize that all is One, that however singular our efforts may seem, we are all bound together in the infinity of our Creator. We will need the strength and comfort of this realization when we come to the Valley of Bewilderment, a place of confusion and pain. Every life has its periods of sorrow and disappointment, times when we feel we have lost our way. It is tempting to give up and drop out, but the support of a faith community and encouragement from fellow travelers can keep us flying toward the goal.

There is yet one more valley to cross before we meet the Simorgh, and that may be the most daunting one of all: the Valley of Death. This is not only the death of the false self but also our physical death. Exhausted by the (hopefully) long years of life with all its dramas and traumas, weakened in body and emptied of all but our sacred essence, we finally come face-to-face with the Object of our lifelong search.

This is the journey the hoopoe describes for the chattering birds. Many perish along the way, but at the end thirty exhausted and tattered birds arrive at the palace of the Simorgh. There they are vetted by a celestial gatekeeper, who reads the trembling birds a record of their lifetime deeds and misdeeds and then finally ushers them into the presence of the Simorgh. The birds watch in astonishment as the final veils of ignorance are lifted and the Light of Lights is manifested. And then, in a magical moment expressed by a Persian play on words (si means thirty and morgh means birds), they grasp the true meaning of their longing for the Simorgh: There in the Simorgh's radiant face they see themselves! In a state of rapture they realize that they are the Simorgh and that the Simorgh is the thirty birds! An inner voice explains that the Simorgh is a majestic mirror and all who come in the presence of Splendor see themselves, their own unique reality. Their long life's journey is at an end, and at last they manifest their truest selves as they dissolve into the Simorgh like a shadow overtaken by the Sun.

Attar concludes his long poem with one last couplet of advice: "And I too cease: I have described the Way. Now you must act—there is no more to say."

REFLECTIONS

✦ Ask yourself honestly, "What excuses do I make to avoid the spiritual journey?" Take inventory of your strengths and weaknesses, and make a conscious commitment to begin the journey, one wing-flap at a time.

✦ Is there a "hoopoe" in your life—someone who can guide and encourage you on the journey? If not, try to find a teacher or at least a fellow traveler to help navigate the mountains and valleys of life as gracefully as possible.

PRACTICE

Attar's poetic imagery lends itself to visual expression in the form of mandalas and labyrinths. Many spiritual traditions use these or other configurations, such as the ornate calligraphy of Qur'anic verses, as aids to meditation and spiritual reflection. If you live near a labyrinth, try walking it step by step with the intention of cleansing your heart along the meandering path in the center. If physically walking a labyrinth is not a possibility, select a mandala or a meaningful piece of Arabic calligraphy to help focus your mind on the journey to your heart's true desire. If you are drawn to artistic expression, you could draw your own mandala or color the ones in books that have been published for that purpose, but remember to keep your focus on the inner journey, not on the art itself.

"In the Name of God, Boundlessly Compassionate and Infinitely Merciful"

(QUR'ANIC INVOCATION)

THESE WORDS, WHICH MUSLIMS UTTER TO THEMSELVES whenever they begin any undertaking, express the very heart of Islamic spirituality. Virtually all 114 chapters of the Qur'an open with this invocation, known as the *Basmala*. The centrality of this sacred formula was proclaimed by Prophet Muhammad, who said that all revelation is contained in the Qur'an, all of the Qur'an is contained in its opening chapter, called the *Fatiha,* and all of the *Fatiha* is contained in the *Basmala.*

To truly understand the secret of this sacred formula, it helps to know a little bit of Arabic. As recited by Muslims, the *Basmala* goes, "*Bismillah ir Rahman ir Rahim.*" The word *Bismillah* is a contraction, meaning "In the name of Allah," and the two words *rahman* and *rahim* are variations on "compassion" and "mercy." But more important, they are extensions of the Semitic root *rhm,* which in both Arabic and Hebrew means "womb." Thus, "compassion" refers to an emanation from a deep, womblike interior, suggesting that this is the mother of all divine attributes. The secret, then, is that it is in the womb of mercy and compassion that our divine identity slowly emerges, and any effort to realize and manifest our sacred essence must begin with the practice of that most elemental of all divine attributes.

Compassion is manifested in many ways, as we have already seen, but here let us focus on this sacred quality as it is expressed through mercy and loving-kindness. The model for divine mercy is the story of God's forgiveness when Adam and his spouse heeded the whispers of Satan and approached the forbidden tree (2:35). As punishment they were banished from the Garden and condemned to a difficult life on Earth, but when they realized that "We have wronged our own souls" (7:23), the All-Merciful One forgave them and exalted them by appointing them and their descendants as God's representatives on Earth (2:30). This story, which is so fundamental not only to Muslims but also to Jews and Christians, teaches two powerful lessons. The first is that when we follow the dictates of our lower selves in defiance of moral standards or our better inclinations, we are essentially wronging our own souls. The second is that once we come to our senses, our Creator, who has never stopped loving us, will forgive us. But the question is this: Can we forgive ourselves?

The Majesty and Beauty of Compassion

Islamic spirituality focuses on the abiding need to understand the majesty and beauty of compassion, and to practice it in our inner and outer lives. Bereft of mercy and gentleness with self, it is difficult to transform the ego and open the heart; without compassion for others, life becomes dreary and burdensome. A Bedouin once pleaded with the Prophet to reveal to him how the *Basmala* might be bestowed on him, and the Prophet replied that when we are compassionate with ourselves and others, the grace of Infinite Compassion will be bestowed upon us.

The transformative powers of compassion are easily illustrated by the element of water in nature. The Qur'an calls it the best metaphor or "sign" of divine compassion. "O my people! Ask forgiveness of your Lord and turn to Him [in repentance]: He will send you the skies pouring abundant rain, and add strength to your strength" (11:52). The special power of that phrase, *add strength to your strength,* can best be appreciated in the context of another Qur'anic verse revealing that water is the very essence of life: "We made from water every living thing" (21:30). In other words, the water of divine compassion adds strength to our sacred essence; it makes us even more of what we already are.

We merely have to observe the effects of water in nature to realize that it is indeed a perfect metaphor for compassion. In a gentle rain, water is soft and yielding, even life-giving: It mists the flowers and cools the skin on a sultry day. "Thou canst see the Earth dry and lifeless—and [suddenly] when we send down waters upon it, it stirs and swells and puts forth every kind of lovely plant!" (22:5). But just as it is easy to underestimate the power of water, so too is it easy to undervalue the power of compassion. In torrents, water has the power to wash away continents; and in "torrents," compassion has the power to wash away the detritus of the false, self-protective ego. In fact, Sufi teachers say that those who are gentle and merciful are the ones who have authentic power. They are the ones who most emulate the life-affirming power of our Creator: "He is the One that sends down rain [even] after [men] have given up all hope, and scatters His Mercy" (42:28).

Compassion for Self

Clearly, then, compassion for self and others is the foundation for all other spiritual practices. But it is axiomatic that we can only truly be compassionate with others when we have learned how to be compassionate with ourselves. The following reflections and practices are useful in developing this life-giving attribute for our own precious souls.

✧✧✧

REFLECTIONS
AND
PRACTICE

If we seek to tame the ego and align it with our higher self by sheer willpower, the ego will resist our efforts with creative excuses for maintaining the status quo. But if we focus the light of awareness on the ego with mercy and gentleness, the ego slowly begins to relent and allows itself to be transformed, just as the hardest stone eventually yields to a steady trickle of water. The three practices described here are the ones that my friends and congregants have found most effective in their work to cultivate the gentle but essential art of compassion for self.

LOVING THE HEART

In an exquisite revelation that came to the Prophet Muhammad in a dream, God said to him, "Neither my Heaven nor my Earth can contain me, but the soft, humble heart of my believing slave can contain me." Think of it: The divine Heart of the All-Compassionate God dwells in the chambers of the human heart! Sages and poets tell us that the human heart yearns to open the window of the heart and gaze incessantly upon the Beloved. It begs to become illumined with love, compassion, light, and delight.

Loving the Heart is a meditative practice that will help build awareness of this heart-to-Heart connection. In silence, focus your attention on your physical heart. With your consciousness, embrace your heart. Remind yourself that the Beloved resides in that space. Then, when you are ready, tell your heart, "I love you." Say the words with feeling—with humility and sincerity. You might also want to say, "Thank you. I am so grateful." Choose words that resonate with you. If it feels narcissistic to say "I love you" to your own heart, remind yourself that the words are directed to Divinity. It may feel awkward at first, but persist with it. Very often, the discomfort dissolves. Spiritual teachers say that as you continue with this practice, a mysterious, divine vibration goes from the tongue into the mouth, into the throat, into the chest, deep into the heart, deeper still into the hidden, and then into the "hidden of the hidden," healing and empowering your sacred essence. Faithful practitioners have reported that in times of difficulty or affliction, they have been astonished to hear a reassuring voice rising from within and telling them the same words that they have repeated so often: "I love you."

SACRED NAMING

Of all the relationships we experience in our lives, the most fundamental one and yet the most neglected is the relationship with our own dear selves. Without our even realizing it, we talk to ourselves often and, sadly, much of this self-talk is quite negative. We castigate ourselves for not being smart enough, quick enough, beautiful enough—the list is long and hurtful. If we are serious about pursuing a relationship with our sacred essence, it is helpful to become more aware of our internal dialogue and practice "spiritual intervention" to transform our negative self-talk by addressing ourselves with affection and compassion.

One of the most effective ways of doing this is a simple practice called Sacred Naming, in which we soften our self-criticisms by directing them not to our "stupid" selves but to our "child of grace" selves. Choose your own term of endearment, something like "Sweetheart," "Dear One," "Brother + your name" (for example, I say, "Brother Jamal"), or whatever feels genuine and evokes compassion for yourself. It may be a loving nickname used by a treasured grandparent or a favorite aunt. The key is to find a sacred name that brings up feelings of mercy and gentleness. Know that there is sacred beauty and power in being named with affection. If the naming is said in a tone of voice that emanates from the heart, it creates a sacred vibration that leaves an indelible imprint on your soul. Recall the sweet vibration of, say, your grandmother's voice when she called you by a pet name with the energy of love and kindness. That is the sweetness we need to use when addressing ourselves.

Having chosen your sacred name, be on the lookout for any opportunity to use it. The moment you become aware that your internal dialogue is beating up on you, immediately intervene by addressing yourself with your sacred name and continue the conversation with the gentler energy that it evokes. Whenever I interject the heartfelt name *Brother Jamal,* I feel a wave of mercy come over me, and I reinforce that feeling by saying, "Brother Jamal, I'm so sorry you're experiencing difficult feelings right now. Please know that I am here to support you," or words to that effect. Invariably, the direction and content of the negative inner conversation change for the good.

Friends and congregants who perform this practice report several major shifts. The sharpness of the ego palpably begins to soften and the ego actually enjoys the moments of collaboration with the soul. Also, there is the added benefit that with continuous practice, you will find yourself naturally naming others with kindness, and this often results in outer harmony and cooperation.

SACRED HOLDING

Perhaps the greatest meaning of compassion for self is that we give ourselves permission to embrace not only our happy feelings but also our difficult ones. The latter have an uncomfortable edge only because we want to keep them separated from us. Difficult feelings, such as anger, pride, and envy, are begging to be acknowledged, embraced, healed, and integrated. All feelings are sacred, says the Qur'an: It is our Creator who grants our laughter and tears (53:43) and who has created for us the faculties of hearing, sight, feeling, and understanding—but "Little thanks it is ye give!" (23:78). Indeed, we tend to give no thanks at all for our difficult feelings. Instead, we try to ignore them, disown them, or act them out in ways that not only hurt others but also harm and embarrass ourselves.

The perfect antidote to this unhelpful tendency is a healing practice called Sacred Holding, which involves acknowledging painful feelings and embracing them with tenderness and compassion, thereby transforming them into a valuable source of self-knowledge, empowerment, and blessing. Sacred Holding is a six-step process that is best done close to the time when you have experienced a painful feeling. But to ensure that you have the technique "at your fingertips" the moment you need it, study these steps and practice them at the earliest opportunity.

1. Give yourself permission to feel your feelings, no matter how difficult or awkward. If possible, ever so gently magnify them, but make sure not to overdo it. Do this little by little, always with compassion for self. Remind yourself that all feelings are sacred.

2. Ask yourself, "Where do I hold this feeling in my body?" Feelings have a resting place, and we experience them as sensations in the physical body: the head, the throat, the heart, the solar plexus, the belly—all are likely sites for emotional distress to settle. Patiently direct your consciousness to locating the site of what is called "physical holding."

3. Once you have located the feelings as sensations in your body, acknowledge them with your consciousness, again with mercy for yourself. You can use Sacred Naming to talk to yourself. You might say affectionately, "Dear Heart, I am sorry for the difficult feelings and sensations you are experiencing. Allow me to support you as you grapple with this difficulty." Hold your sensations with the tender embrace of the soul. Continuously shine the light of merciful awareness on them and abide with them. If the sensations move to another location, move your attention to that place. At this time there is no need to fix or analyze the sensations; simply be present with the holding as long as you want. Spiritual guides explain that by doing this, you allow for a "streaming beauty" to flow through you. The Qur'an has a beautiful metaphor for this light of gentle awareness to soften and transmute: It is akin to "the dawn as it breathes away the darkness" (81:18).

4. Lovingly direct some questions to the center of sensations in your body. "Do you have a message for me? Is there a secret you want to share with me?" Simply listen. Be attentive and respectful, even if you hear nothing.

5. Ask tenderly, "How may I befriend you? How may I love you and integrate you?" Again, just listen sincerely.

6. Make an intention to allow your breath to flow through that physical locus of your feelings as you inhale and exhale. Allow the divine Breath to caress that focal point. Little by little, you will experience healing, integration, and transformation of the difficult feelings.

"We Have Made Some of You as a Trial for Others: Will You Have Patience?"

(QUR'AN 25:20)

THIS VERSE FROM THE QUR'AN OFTEN PROMPTS A WRY chuckle, but the question is serious: Can we be patient with each other? More to the point, can we extend to our fellow beings the same generosity and compassion that we are developing for ourselves? Having realized that we are more than mere bundles of conditioned personality—we are the possessors of divine essence—can we also view others as manifestations of the Creator? Islam and its fellow Abrahamic religions, Judaism and Christianity, all say we must. "If I am only for myself," said the great Rabbi Hillel, "what am I?" The prophet Jesus quoted the scripture of his Jewish forebears when he reminded his followers to treat others as themselves—not just as they would like to be treated, but as if they were literally part and parcel of each other. And the Qur'an says we are indeed all infused with the Breath of God, meaning that each one of us is sacred to the core. In a beautiful metaphor by the fourteenth-century Sufi poet Hafiz, we are all guests of honor at a divine banquet. Knowing that each one of us is a guest of honor, Hafiz asks, how would we treat our fellow guests?

Behavior and Being

Once we have begun to see ourselves as manifestations of the Creator, the next step along the spiritual path is to view our fellow beings with the same compassionate eyes. This will seem natural enough in the case of our friends and loved ones, though we still may lapse into self-centered behaviors when our ego-driven personalities collide. It is another thing to extend compassion to a stranger or an enemy who does us harm. That is when the Qur'an calls us to remember that each person is essentially good, or *fitra,* and possessed of divine potential. Rather than focusing on someone's conditioned personality, which may indeed be good or bad, we begin to realize that we are all guests at the same banquet, and the Host sees a sacred essence that may be masked by harmful or unacceptable behaviors. Thus in our interactions with others it is important to distinguish between behavior and being. A person's behavior may sometimes be offensive or evil, but the *person* cannot be evil. Each person's essential being, even a criminal's, is filled with the sacred breath of the Creator.

This is not to say we should simply accept someone's bad behavior and let ourselves be harmed by others. The sixteenth-century Sufi sage Kabir advises us to do what is right, protect ourselves, and don't allow ourselves to be abused. But he entreats us not to keep the other person's being out of our heart. A Sufi story about the sentencing of a miscreant expands on this theme. One judge might proclaim the sentence with contempt, seeing no distinction between the person's essence and his criminal behavior. He is ready to lock the criminal up and throw away the key. Another judge might render the same sentence, but with enough regard for the offender's soul that he specifies conditions to ensure that the convict is accorded human dignity and not maltreated in prison. For the convict, the situation is the same either way: He is going to jail. But Sufis believe the mere fact that a judge would value the offender's essence despite his crime could be the turning point in the criminal's self-perception and start him on a path of rehabilitation and spiritual growth. The compassionate judge, having exercised his capacity for spaciousness toward a fellow human being, makes a conscious distinction between behavior and being. This distinction has the power to shift Heaven and Earth.

When we do not make a distinction between behavior and being, we can lapse into the danger of judging an entire culture or religion based on the behavior of some misguided individuals. We begin to generalize and make blanket condemnations. This affects our behavior and produces hurtful consequences. Unwilling to believe that other persons—or entire peoples—share our same divine essence, we claim a higher moral ground and refuse to engage in dialogue. Worse, we justify and rely on the use of force to make them see things our way. We delude ourselves and keep from seeing the truth to avoid the real work of recognizing and relating to the divine in each other. Aleksandr Solzhenitsyn, the Russian dissident, sums it up succinctly: "If only there were evil people somewhere insidiously committing evil deeds and it were necessary only to separate them from the rest of us and destroy them. But the line dividing good and evil cuts through the heart of every human being. And who is willing to destroy a piece of his own heart?"[1]

Healing the Blinded Heart

We know from our own experiences that when we are treated with compassion and dignity, our hearts respond in harmony and appreciation. But when we are treated with anger or distrust, our hearts clench in self-defense and slam their metaphorical windows shut. This is how people respond when they suffer too long from helplessness and disenfranchisement at the hands of the powerful who discriminate against them or oppress them because of their color, their language, their beliefs, or their social customs. Chronically mistreated and subjugated, they soon become blind to their own sacred essence, let alone that of the oppressor. In the words of the Qur'an, "Truly it is not their eyes that are blind, but their hearts" (22:46).

The reality of blinded hearts is often on display in the Middle East, and I have seen it up close on two trips to Israel and Palestine with my Interfaith Amigos, Rabbi Ted Falcon and Pastor Don Mackenzie. Clearly, the terrible injustices that have been visited on Jews, Arabs, and Palestinians in the course of history have hardened and blinded many hearts on all sides. What will open those hearts? The use of force will only cause hearts to clench even more tightly against the pain. Reason is powerless in the face of passion and emotion. The only key to a locked heart is forged of qualities that the heart recognizes and trusts as its own: compassion, love, forgiveness, and higher understanding. Only that which comes from the heart can open another heart.

What gives us hope are the numerous grassroots movements of unsung heroes and heroines who, with compassion and courage, reach out across the divide. Heartbroken parents of Jewish children killed by Palestinian suicide bombers and of Muslim children killed by Israeli Defense Forces are reaching out to one another and working to end senseless violence. Jewish and Palestinian women, at no little risk to themselves, are collaborating on a handicrafts project to enable the Palestinian women to earn a modicum of financial security for their families. Rabbis and sheikhs, living the heart of their traditions, speak out against injustices and offer solutions based on mercy and fairness. Youths from all sides dare to study, sing, and play together, trying to come up with creative ideas to break the logjam of ignorance and arrogance in their communities.

The challenge—and the opportunity—whenever we find ourselves in situations of polarized "otherness" is to humbly and skillfully create an environment of compassion and trust that will allow the divine identity of the other to come forth. The Qur'an reminds those who would truly worship God that we are to be "a Mercy for all creatures" (21:107)—even if we *are* sometimes a trial to each other. The Prophet Muhammad once was asked to curse idolaters, but he replied, "I was not sent to curse; I was only sent as a mercy." On another occasion he rescued a desert Arab who, not knowing any better, had urinated in the mosque. A disgusted crowd seized the poor man, but the Prophet said to them, "Leave him alone, and pour a bucket of water over what he has passed, for you have been sent only to make things easy, and not to make things difficult." In view of such examples, we are inspired to put into practice in our own lives the injunctions to distinguish between behavior and being, to be just, but not to make life difficult for those who are a trial for us.

REFLECTIONS

- ✦ Consider the spiritual need to distinguish between behavior and being in dealing with someone difficult in your life. How does this impact your speech or actions?
- ✦ Take the Prophet's words to heart: "Make things easy for others." How can you apply this counsel in your life?

PRACTICE

Make it a practice to focus on your heart from time to time and intend to send out light to people around you: the grocery clerk, your office mates, sports teammates, the police officer who stops you for speeding, your loved ones around the dinner table. Imagine a shaft or cord or ray of light pouring in an outward and expansive direction. Initially, you may not feel anything, but with practice you will feel sensations and movement in the center of your chest. Know that the source of your inner light is infinite. When you radiate light toward others, the light within you grows stronger. If the other person happens to be someone you dislike, remind yourself that you are sending light to that person's soul, not his or her personality. Over time, this practice will open your heart more and more, and your relationships will become ever more harmonious and fulfilling.

"Ye Shall Surely Travel from Stage to Stage"

(QUR'AN 84:19)

THE SPIRITUAL ROAD IS LONG—*LIFE*-LONG—AND WE NEED
an occasional rest stop lest we burn out or become too discouraged
to continue. We cannot expect to achieve spiritual enlightenment all
at once. We may indeed have flashes of brilliant insight from time to
time, but by and large the catchphrase in Sufi spirituality is "little by
little." The Holy Qur'an reminds us that we shall attain our goal in
good time: "O human being! Truly, you are laboring toward your
Sustainer, painfully struggling, but then you shall meet Him" (84:6).

The problem is that we humans don't like to delay our gratifica-
tion. We want it all, and we want it now, without having to grind it
out little by little. We are like the Mulla, who became enamored of
Indian classical music and was eager to learn. So he went to the master musician and asked how much it would cost to enroll in classes.
"Three pieces of silver for the first month and one piece of silver from
the second month onward," replied the master. "Very well!" said the
Mulla. "Sign me up from the second month!"

This reminds me of the ironic little prayer, "Dear God, give
me patience—and please grant it to me right now!" We forget

that every saint once struggled to manifest his or her sacred potential and every sinner has a future possibility of joyful connection between personality and essence. Compassionately remind yourself of those words in the Holy Qur'an: "Will you have patience?"(25:20).

And be prepared for beautiful surprises. My friend Kate tells me that spiritual practice reminds her of the moment she saw a Turkish dye master lift a batch of yarn from a vat of indigo. Indigo is a very old and natural dye that does not use a mordant (a fixative) to set the dye. Rather, the dye works by a process of natural fermentation, turning the yarn first yellow and then bright green before magically transforming it into a deep shade of blue once it is exposed to air. For Kate, the indigo process is a perfect metaphor for our spiritual work on several levels. It was developed in antiquity because of humans' love of beauty, just as the spiritual practices in this book have evolved from humans' desire from time immemorial to have a connection with Divinity. It is a natural process that unfolds through a series of necessary steps, just like spiritual growth. Because there is no mordant involved, the dye is not really fixed—your faded blue jeans are proof of that—and our spiritual "dye" is not fixed either: It requires constant attention and corrective steps to keep it fresh and beautiful.

Recalling the Qur'an's promise, mentioned earlier, that "with every difficulty there is relief" (94:5), it is nourishing simply to rest with your heart and take quiet inventory of what you have accomplished thus far. No need to judge—merely be grateful for the steps you have taken and know that the Beloved has taken many more steps toward you. The journey will continue, but for now, just relax and reflect on the assurance of this beautiful Qur'anic verse: "So I call to witness the rosy glow of sunset; the night and its progression; and the moon as it grows into fullness; surely you shall travel from stage to stage" (84:16–19).

REFLECTIONS
AND
PRACTICE

Amazingly, the "little by little" application leads eventually to a quantum leap, and then the cycle starts again. There is incremental progress and then yet another quantum leap. It truly pays to persist little by little. Can you think of a time in your own life when persistent practice led to a major shift in your awareness?

GEM 11

"Will You Not See? Will You Not Listen? Will You Not Pay Attention?"

(QUR'AN 54:17, 7:204)

OVER AND OVER AGAIN, THE QUR'AN, LIKE AN EARNEST parent or a patient teacher, calls us to bear conscious witness to the unfolding of meaning in our inner lives and in the farthest reaches of creation. "We will show them Our signs on the farthest horizons, and in their own selves, until it becomes manifest to them that this is the truth" (41:53). Ours is a mysterious universe and we are asked to awaken to the preciousness of divine Presence in every moment. "If a drop of the wine of vision could rinse our eyes," says our friend Rumi, "everywhere we look we would weep with wonder."

Theoretically, we know how important it is to live in the present, but the truth is that our awareness is often interrupted because our minds are busily flitting back and forth between past regrets and future anxieties. Living in those worlds of past and future, we miss out on the opportunities and gifts of the present moment, what Sufis call the divine party that is always happening in the now. "If you shed tears when you miss the Sun," says the Bengali poet Rabindranath Tagore, "you also miss the stars."[1] The past is over and the future has not yet arrived. The seasons, which the Qur'an cites so often as signs of God's presence and action in our lives, have their own distinct names. Spring is not called "postwinter," and winter is not called "prespring." Only by fully participating in the seasons as they occur can we experience and enjoy each season for what it is.

Attention to the Moment

The preciousness of the moment is well illustrated by the story of a Buddhist monk who suffers from a terrible toothache. "Oh," he groans, "if only this toothache would go away, I would be a happy man." Suddenly he gets an insight and is eager to share it with his fellow monks, who seem much too preoccupied with the seriousness of life. "Do you have a toothache?" he asks them one by one. "No? Then why aren't you happy? Don't you realize that this very moment is a nontoothache moment?" How many nontoothache moments have we glided through without the slightest awareness, appreciation, or enjoyment of them? "Will you not see" how beautifully your body functions? "Will you not hear" how faithfully your heart beats? "Will you not pay attention" to the breath you took just now? For most of us, it takes a heart scare or a bout of pneumonia to remind us not to take these precious gifts for granted—and even then, how long do we stay aware?

Just as we ignore our physical faculties, we also tend to ignore our material blessings, wanting more and forgetting to appreciate what we already have. "Man does not weary of asking for good things" (41:49), says the Qur'an, and it chides us for taking "things" as our due. In our vague dissatisfaction, we are like the seeker who packed his belongings in a knapsack and set off in search of happiness. On the way he met the Mulla and told him of his discontent. Suddenly, the Mulla grabbed the man's knapsack and ran off with it. "Stop!" cried the man as he ran after the Mulla. "Those are my life possessions! Stop!" The Mulla stopped abruptly and handed over the bag. With a sense of relief the man exclaimed, "I feel so happy to have my things back!" The Mulla gave him an amused look and said, "Before you get angry at me, please notice that you feel happy. You had the possessions before I took them from you, but you were not grateful for them. You were not present with the joy of what you possessed until you lost it. May you learn to treasure the blessings of what you have."

This insight resonated with me when a friend asked to borrow a book from my personal library. I was happy to lend him any book he asked for, but suddenly this particular book became precious to me, even though it had been lying unnoticed on the shelf for several years! I was eager for my friend to return the book, and I really enjoyed rereading it before replacing it on the dusty shelf. As a result of that experience, I have a little ritual of touching and thanking my books from time to time and rereading selected portions. Instead of waiting to be happy when the next new book arrives, I am happy now with the old friends in my library.

The Practice of Living in the Moment

Does the commitment to living in the moment mean that we should forget the past and ignore the future? Of course not! We need to learn from our past experiences and plan for future needs. The problem comes when we allow ourselves to flit from one tense to another without being conscious of where we are right now. Our minds are everywhere and nowhere—a psychological displacement that is both physically and spiritually exhausting. What is called for is a clear intention to focus consciously on the issue at hand and give ourselves permission to dwell on it for a specific amount of time.

For example, whenever I catch my mind continually veering away from the present moment to dwell on some past regret, I tell myself compassionately, "Brother Jamal, I notice that something is bothering you and you are not present. Let's resolve this now. I give you permission to think and feel your past regrets fully and freely for, say, the next twenty minutes." This "allowing" makes me present with my past regrets. The past becomes graced with energies of the present and often I glean useful insights from the past. I use the same technique of self-talk to be present with my anxieties about the future. I might say, "Brother Jamal, I give you twenty minutes to worry as much as you want to about this issue." When the allotted time is over, I return myself gently but firmly to the present moment.

Negative Imaginary Scenarios

It is important to exercise control over the quality of our thoughts and feelings because, as Tagore puts it, they deliver unseen chisel blows toward the sculpting of our destiny. It is amazing how our thoughts shape our lives. Rumi says that if our thoughts circle a ruby mine, we become a ruby; if they circle food, we become a loaf of bread; if they circle money, we can be bought and sold. The vibrations of feelings affect our souls. An abundance of life-affirming feelings stirs the soul and prompts us to act in positive, uplifting ways. An excess of unpleasant feelings bruises the soul, especially if these feelings flow from what Sufis call negative imaginary scenarios in the landscape of our minds and hearts. If through our fertile imagination we continuously play out these negative scenarios internally, they manifest on some level of reality. The subconscious cannot distinguish between real and imagined scenarios, so it absorbs and reacts to the negativity as if it were real, triggering a downward spiral of depression and hopelessness. Thus it is critical to become aware of these negative imaginary scenarios swirling in our minds and to intervene immediately. Sufis say, *"Tauba! Tauba!"* the moment they recognize this happening. The word *tauba* implies the intention to turn to God for help. Buddhist practitioners reject the scenario altogether, saying, *"Neti! Neti"* or "Not real! Not real!" The cybersavvy may bridge the two approaches, acknowledging the scenario but turning away from it by saying, "Cancel! Cancel!" or "Delete! Delete!" Any of these spiritual interventions will break the pattern and, by the grace of God, allow space for beautiful patterns of thoughts and feelings to take root.

The Art of Being in the Present

Some of the most powerful lessons I have learned about the art of being present have occurred while visiting friends who were terminally ill. I particularly remember my good friend Janet Turner, who lived for a number of years on borrowed time with a transplanted kidney. Filled with gratitude and intensely mindful about time, she constantly asked herself, "What is it that I would truly like to accomplish, experience, and express to others?" She traveled extensively, took countless classes, volunteered to help complete innumerable projects, and tended her relationships with family and friends. Eventually, the transplanted kidney began to fail, and Janet felt her life force ebbing away. Although disabled by pain and weakness, she continued to nourish her soul by listening to chants and music and by reflecting on verses of insight and beauty from sacred texts and sublime poetry. Two weeks before she died, she softly held my hands in hers and said with utmost honesty and clarity, "Thank you from the core of my heart for your words and chants, but what I really need from you is for you to be present. That is your best gift to me." I asked her to tell me more. She explained, "If you feel awkward, feel awkward. That is healing to me. If you feel like crying, cry. That is healing to me. If you are speechless, don't say anything. Be silent. That is healing to me. If you feel you really want to tell me something, talk to me. Your words are healing to me." She said many more words along the same lines and in that moment I began to grasp something of what it means to be present and authentic. Thanks to Janet, I am blessed with a slight knowing of the mystery that the present moment is suffused with, the fragrance of the divine.

REFLECTIONS
AND
PRACTICE

The Sufis have a saying, "A Sufi is a son or daughter of the present moment." Whenever you realize you have strayed unconsciously into the past or future, immediately intervene with compassionate self-talk. "Dear one," you might say, "will you not see? Will you not listen? Will you not pay attention?" And then remind yourself of that Sufi saying, that you are a son or daughter of the present moment.

To help build your ability to stay grounded in the present moment, try these two meditations:

✦ Close your eyes and bring your attention to rest on your heart. Go deeper into that space, and begin to connect with your heart. Listen to your heartbeat and repeat a life-affirming word or verse with gratitude for the present moment. Stay with this for a few minutes.

✦ With your eyes closed, focus on the lowest part of the spine, the sacrum area, and from there intend to send a beautiful cord of light deep into the Earth. Take the light even deeper and feel this shaft of light connecting you to the womb of Mother Earth. Feel a sense of rootedness and grounding. Spend some time here. Shift your focus now to the crown of your head. From there, send out a cord of light traveling upward, piercing the mysterious realms and connecting you to the heart of Heaven. Feel a protective bonding with the dimensions of Mystery. Again, spend some time just savoring this connection. If you wish, chant or repeat sacred verses into that space, and use those same chants to remind yourself to stay centered and mindful throughout the day.

PURIFYING AND EXPANDING THE HEART

"O My Lord! Open for Me My Heart!"

(QUR'AN 20:25)

DURING THE QUESTION-AND-ANSWER SESSION FOL-
lowing a presentation some years ago, a no-nonsense woman
demanded to know why I talked so much about focusing on the
heart. "It's just an anatomical organ," she said. Ah, but what an
organ! In Islamic spirituality the heart is the metaphoric center of
our deepest longings, highest aspirations, most exalted wisdom,
and infinitely unbounded love. The Qur'an says that when God
charged the prophet Moses with delivering the Israelites from
bondage in Egypt, Moses's first request was not for practical assistance with this overwhelming task but for the gift of spiritual
insight: "O my Lord! Open for me my heart!" (20:25). Similarly,
when we first awaken to our spiritual longings, we can almost
hear our hearts crying out to be opened, expanded, and filled
with divine Presence. How could it be otherwise? Divine Heart,
according to a hadith qudsi, already is in human heart! What we
are longing for is to break through the levels of ego that veil our
hearts from seeing and experiencing the radiance of the divine
Heart within.

Polishing the Heart

A primary way to open the heart is to purify our being. Sufi teachers tell us that it is imperative for us to strive to polish our hearts. The Qur'an warns us, "On their hearts is the stain of the ill which they do! Verily from the Light of their Lord … will they be veiled" (83:14–15). With this Sufi practice, the cleansed heart becomes like a polished mirror that reflects the beauty of Allah. As we polish the veils away, our being is pierced by a sweet, divine light and we experience joy, tranquility, and inner strength. The eyes of our hearts open and we gain access to the secrets of the invisible world.

During one of the Mulla's lectures on polishing the heart to reveal the mysteries of God and invisible realms, a skeptical student challenged him, "If all this is true, show us something from those celestial realms." The Mulla immediately reached for an apple from the fruit basket and handed it to him. "But this has imperfections," complained the student. "This is not a celestial apple." "You're right," replied the Mulla, "but given your present state of corruption, this is the closest you will ever come to a heavenly apple!" To know something higher, we have to first reach a higher state. We cannot begin to glimpse the divine loveliness unless our own being first becomes lovely. The Mystery reveals itself only to the degree to which we have overcome our faults and polished our hearts so that they mirror the Beloved.

What does this work of purification involve? Two things, say the sages—diminishing our ego attributes and deepening our divine qualities. Within us is a jungle, says Rumi, where the fair and foul both roam. Our work is to diminish the foul and expand on the fair, for, as Rumi reminds us, we are whatever dominates within us. If our gold outweighs our copper, we will be known as gold.

Spiritual teachers advise us not to be overwhelmed by what seems to be the enormity of the work of purification. When we diminish one ego trait, other ego traits also begin to fade. Likewise, if we deepen one divine virtue, we enhance others. Everything within and without is profoundly interconnected. To help open hearts, Sufi teachers work with individual students to deepen specific divine attributes according to their personality needs. Among the many attributes chosen by the teacher, the most common ones are patience, humility, sincerity, and truthfulness.

The Prophet Muhammad said, "For every rust there is a polish, and the polish of the heart is the remembrance of God."[1] Rumi's favorite way of polishing the heart was a type of *zikr* (from the Arabic root meaning "remembrance") practiced by whirling dervishes, a spiritual order that he instituted in the thirteenth century. In this sacred dance, the practitioner focuses on the physical heart to remember the divine Indweller while rotating the body and occasionally making the motions of polishing the heart. The veils between heart and Heart dissolve as the dervish turns, and the human heart of the dervish experiences joy and ecstasy in feeling close to the divine Heart. When we polish our heart with such remembrance, whether by sacred dancing or by other practices such as chanting and meditation, our heart truly begins to open up.

REFLECTIONS

The beloved ninth-century sage Rabia cried out, "There is a disease in my breast no doctor can cure. Only union with the Friend can cure it."[2]

Have you ever felt an unexplained sadness, loneliness, or yearning inside you? Is it possible to embrace the feeling with compassion and mercy for yourself?

PRACTICE

A beloved Sufi practice for polishing the heart is to sit quietly for a few moments, focusing on the heart, and then gently sway back and forth (rather like Jewish *davening*) and make polishing motions on the chest while reciting the word *Estaghfirullah*, which means "I beg repentance, Allah." Christians will recognize the similarity of this word to the Jesus Prayer (also known, aptly enough, as the "Prayer of the Heart"): "Lord Jesus Christ, have mercy on me, a sinner." The idea with either the Muslim or the Christian prayer is not to berate oneself, but to caress the heart space with compassion for self and with love for the Heart within your heart. One begs forgiveness for being unaware or forgetful of the divine Heart dwelling in the human heart.

"Bring to God a Sound Heart"

(QUR'AN 26:89)

WHETHER CONSCIOUSLY OR NOT, ALL OF US ARE "JOUR-neying to God" (35:18), and the work we are doing to purify our hearts will stand us in good stead on Judgment Day. On that day only those who "bring to God a sound heart" will prosper, so truly, "whoever purifies himself does so for the benefit of his own soul" (35:18). We already know the journey will be long and unpredictable, so it would be wise to travel light. Look into your baggage, says Rumi, and discern whether the contents are worth bringing along. Remove the bitter ones and "redeem yourself from fruitless effort and disgrace." Bring only your divine qualities, such as compassion, honesty, and joy. Or, as the Qur'an says, "Bring a heart that can respond" (50:33).

What are some of the bitter contents that we need to remove? The Prophet is said to have taught, "There are three things at the root of all sin. Guard yourself against them and beware of them. Beware of pride, for pride caused *Iblis* to refuse to prostrate himself before Adam. Beware of greed, for greed caused Adam to eat of the tree. And beware of envy, for it was from envy that one of the two sons of Adam killed his brother."[1] Two other ego qualities that also weigh heavily in our baggage are anger and fear. All these qualities emanate from an untamed ego.

Pride: The Obstacle of Self-Righteousness

When we do not work to transform our ego, we puff up with pride and have a highly exaggerated opinion of ourselves. We are like the Mulla, who peered into a well one night and was horrified to discover the Moon lying at the bottom. "This is a disaster for the world," he thought to himself, and he rushed home to get a rope. After tying a hook to one end, he flung the rope into the well. "Worry not, Sister Moon," he cooed. "Help is at hand." The hook seemed to have gotten hold of a part of the Moon. The Mulla heaved with all his might, and as the hook loosened something in the bottom of the well, he fell on his back, from which position he was able to see the Moon restored to its proper domain. "Thank God I came along," said the Mulla to himself. "Imagine the consequences if I had not been here to rescue the Moon!"

An insidious danger along the spiritual path is the temptation to become proud and self-righteous about our holiness, especially when we see others acting in ways of which we disapprove. Sages caution against fiery indignation and our tendency to excuse it as a reasonable defense of truth or justice. Do respond appropriately if it is warranted, they advise, but do not think of yourself as pure, or revile others, for the only sins you need to account for are your own. "Is it not enough," asks the Qur'an, "that your Sustainer is a witness to all things?" (41:53).

Greed: Trying to Satisfy the Ego

It is in the nature of the commanding ego always to want more and more. It is never satisfied. Sufis say that the transformed egos of two dervishes are content to share a loaf of bread and one blanket, whereas a king with an imperial ego conspires day and night to enlarge his kingdom and enrich his coffers even more. Or, as the eighth-century renowned scholar Imam Jafar Sadiq once put it, "If the son of Adam were to possess two valleys of gold and silver, he would long for a third."[2] The Qur'an has harsh words for hoarders who "bury gold and silver and spend it not in the way of Allah" (9:34). Theirs shall be "a most grievous penalty" for their sinful selfishness. By all means enjoy beautiful things and good food, says the Holy Book, but don't go overboard, "for God loveth not the wasters" (7:31).

The antidote for greed is to come to a heartfelt realization that nothing of the created world will ever fully satisfy the ego. Only that which is of divine essence will truly satisfy us. What will slake our thirst are divine qualities, such as love, compassion, beauty, faith, freedom, and joy. "That which is from the presence of God is better than any bargain or passing delight! For God is the best of providers" (62:11).

Envy: Mischief of the Ego

An untamed ego enjoys feeling superior. The success of others arouses jealousy. Such an ego is inclined, consciously or unconsciously, to denigrate the other through the mischief of words and deeds.

The penultimate chapter of the Qur'an, just five verses long, contains instructions for protecting ourselves from the damage that envy can do: "Say: I seek refuge with the Lord of the Dawn ... from the mischief of the envious one as he practices envy" (113:1, 5). And to help those of us who feel envy and jealousy because others seem to have been more favored, the Qur'an reminds us that on Judgment Day "neither wealth nor children" will influence Allah (26:88–89). Only those who have been conscious of God and engaged in righteous deeds will have a heavenly reward.

Anger: Fire of Satan

The unchecked anger of the ego can be all-consuming, and is therefore dangerous to oneself and others.

Someone once asked the Prophet to convey a teaching that was essential but brief and to the point. The Prophet replied, "Do not become angry and furious." The man asked again and again, and each time the Prophet answered back with the same words: "Do not become angry and furious." This anecdote illustrates the great need to understand and cope with our anger. The energy of anger is fiery and powerful. Rumi calls it a "king over kings," but goes on to say that, once bridled, it might serve the cause of good. How do we soften the raging fire of anger before it overwhelms us? In addition to prayer, the Prophet had a practical suggestion: Upon feeling rage, immediately perform ablution with water, for "anger is from Satan, Satan is from fire, and water extinguishes fire."

Fear: Growing Stronger with Denial

The vibrations of fear weigh heavily on us, especially when we avoid and deny them. Fear grows in the dark, both literally and figuratively. Shadows assume frightening shapes, and we begin to live in a trance of fear. But our feelings of fear, just like our negative feelings, simply want to be acknowledged and embraced. Looking compassionately at our fears little by little dissolves the burden of the trance. Sufi teachers especially warn us not to create fear in others in order to manipulate them. Such is the volatile energy of fear that it also overwhelms the being of the manipulator. A mother once brought her young son to the Mulla and asked him to put fear into the heart of her son, who had become rebellious and intransigent. The Mulla looked fiercely into the eyes of the son, commanded him to listen to his mother, and then proceeded to contort his face into a monstrous shape and let out a frightening growl. He appeared and sounded so fearsome that the mother fainted and the Mulla rushed out of the room. When the mother regained consciousness, she berated the Mulla, "I asked you to scare my son, not me!" "Madam," replied the Mulla, "fear has no favorites. It consumes everyone. You might not have noticed, but I myself got so scared that I had to leave the room!"

REFLECTIONS

What are some specific negative ego traits in yourself that you would like to curb and contain?

PRACTICE

Keep a small notebook in your pocket and record the ego qualities that you see yourself manifesting in the course of the day. Review them each evening and express gratitude to God for your growing awareness of these traits that need to be diminished. At the end of the week, create a ritual of purification and release. For example, you could write down the traits, put the list in a fireproof bowl, and burn it with a prayer for divine assistance in the coming week. Or you could write the list with water-soluble ink, place the list in a bowl of water, and watch gratefully as the unwanted traits dissolve before your very eyes.

GEM 14

"Who Has a Better Dye Than God?"

(QUR'AN 2:138)

LITTLE DID MY FRIEND KATE REALIZE, AS SHE WATCHED that Turkish dye master with his vats of indigo, that she was witnessing a process that has long been a favorite Sufi metaphor for the acquisition of sacred attributes. Dip fabric into a vat of dye, and it will take on a beautiful color; leave it for a while, and the color will intensify. But when exposed to the wear and tear of daily life the dye will fade, so the process must be repeated regularly to keep the color strong. "Who has a better dye than God?" asks the Qur'an. Sufis say that, with persistent "dipping" into that dye, our heart will take on a sacred hue over time. To dip into that dye means to infuse our heart with the divine qualities found in the manifold Names of God.

To God belong ninety-nine beautiful names, says the Islamic tradition, and according to the Qur'an, patience is one of the most essential virtues to have in our spiritual knapsack. We shall consider this in more detail now, followed by three other important virtues mentioned often in the Holy Book: humility, sincerity, and truthfulness.

Patience

"You shall most certainly be tried in your possessions and in your persons," says the Qur'an, "... But if you remain patient in adversity and conscious of Him—this, behold, is something to set one's heart upon" (3:186). Mere endurance will not suffice to bring ease to the heart. You will soon become impatient with your patience! Induce the presence of Divinity in your endurance so that your patience becomes holy patience. "Seek help with patient perseverance and prayer: for God is with those who patiently persevere" (2:153).

Unfortunately for us, patience is not a virtue that we can simply say "Be!" and it is, even for saints and prophets. Early in his mission, the Prophet Muhammad lamented to God that he had not received a divine revelation in many months and he was beginning to feel lonely and neglected. Finally came a revelation: "By the Glorious Morning Light, and by the Night when it is still, thy Guardian Lord hath not forsaken thee" (93:1–3). God asks Muhammad to be patient and assures him, "Verily the hereafter will be better for thee than the present" (93:4). Qur'anic scholars explain that *hereafter* in this passage does not refer to the afterlife, but to each succeeding moment in life, which becomes enriched with increased understanding and spiritual growth.

Other revelations suggest that Muhammad did not find it easy to be patient with those who aggressively mocked his message and tried to destroy his community. "We know indeed the grief which their words do cause thee" (6:33) came one such revelation, but "rejected were the apostles before thee: with patience and constancy they bore their rejection and their wrongs" (6:34). It would do the Prophet no good to tunnel into the ground or climb a ladder to the skies to bring God's word to the ignorant, continues the revelation, "So be not thou among those who are swayed by ignorance and impatience!" (6:35).

It is especially hard to be patient when we first begin the spiritual journey, for we are eager to make up for lost time (a worthy objective) and also maybe to outshine our fellow travelers (not so worthy).

One such aspirant sought out a well-known teacher and asked how long the course would take. "Ten years" was the reply—far too long for the aspirant. What if he studied twice as hard? "Twenty years," replied the teacher. By now confused, the student asked what if he studied three times harder. "Thirty years," said the teacher. "Why is it," asked the student, "that every time I propose to work harder, you tell me it will take longer?" "Simple," said the master. "When one eye is constantly fixed on your ambition of tinsel and glitter in this world, there is only one eye left with which to find your way. The path of spirituality requires patience, humility, sincerity, and pure intentions."

Humility

The son of a reputed Sufi teacher was eager to train under his father, but was told that first he must be apprenticed to a teacher who lived in a distant village. The young man was reluctant to follow this path, for he assumed that a village sheikh would be far less qualified and worthy of respect than his esteemed father, but he made his way to the sheikh and dutifully bowed in obeisance. "Lower!" shouted the peasant master. The young man hunched down. "Not enough! Lower! Lower still!" the teacher commanded. In the course of this apprenticeship, by bending lower and lower still, the young man cracked the proud shell of his ego. Only then was he ready to study with his father.

This story illustrates the power of a physical posture that is central to Islamic spirituality. Several times a day observant Muslims perform the *salat,* the ritual prayer that involves falling on one's knees before Allah and touching one's forehead to the floor in deep humility. The simple act of lowering the head and bowing to God reinforces over and over again an acknowledgment of something infinitely greater than the self-centered ego. This gesture, when done consciously, brings us ever closer to the Divinity at our core, so that in surrendering our pride we grow in true dignity. We become like the raindrop in a poem by the thirteenth-century sage Saadi of Shiraz. When the raindrop, dripping from a cloud, saw the sea, it blushed and exclaimed, "Who am I in the presence of the sea?" Deeply moved by the raindrop's humility, an oyster took it into its heart, and fate so shaped its destiny that eventually the raindrop became a precious pearl.

For many Muslims, the prime model of humility is the Prophet Muhammad. In the seventh century, when people wanted to kiss his hands, he reminded them that he was not a king and that "I am only a mortal, just like you." When people overly praised him, he said, "Don't exceed bounds in praising me; I am only the Lord's servant; then call me the servant of God and His messenger."

Sincerity

The Prophet Muhammad told his followers that in a moment of personal revelation God said to him, "Sincerity is a secret taken from My secret. I have placed it as a trust in the hearts of servants I love." To get a sense of divine sincerity, teachers ask us to reflect on the signs of God in nature. Whether we give thanks to God or not, every day without fail we are blessed with the beauty of sunrise and sunset— and the Sun, Hafiz tells us, never says, "You owe me!" Soil and seeds are faithful to their trust: Plant a mango seed in the soil, and a mango tree grows. The waters of mercy descend on the orchards of rich and poor alike. Spring comes and flowers blossom. There is a deep and vital trust in nature that we take for granted. Such is the awesome sincerity of God.

In light of such sincerity, the least we can do is keep our promises. Odious to God is the fact that we so often say one thing and do another, says the Qur'an (61:2–3), and the Holy Book advises us at every stage of life to pray, "O my Sustainer! Cause me to enter upon whatever I may do in a true and sincere way, and cause me to complete it in a true and sincere way" (17:80). Sadly, the ego sometimes compromises our sincerity by finding creative ways to avoid fulfilling our commitments and promises.

The Mulla, by now a wealthy man, had a life-threatening illness and prayed fervently for divine help, in return for which he would sell one of his million-dollar houses and donate the proceeds to the poor. Miraculously, his illness disappeared! The Mulla felt committed to honoring his promise but was reluctant to give away such a large sum, so he thought of a way to get around it. He placed a copy of the Qur'an in the house and in his advertisement stipulated that the Holy Book was an integral part of the sale. The price of the house was affixed at half a million dollars and the Qur'an also at half a million. Upon sale of the house, he gave to charity the amount paid for the house and pocketed the amount paid for the Qur'an. "I have fulfilled my promise," he said to himself: "Thank God for creative solutions!"

The depth of our sincerity is a direct reflection of our state of consciousness. The higher the state, the more authentic is our sincerity. The more persistently we work to realize and manifest our sacred essence, the more soul-like does our sincerity become. That is why teachers make a distinction between sincerity of personality and sincerity of soul. The former is limited by conditionings and rigidities of the personality, while the latter has a quality of an open heart and mind—it embodies something of the fragrance of God. In a well-loved story on this theme, a famous religious teacher and three disciples traveled far up a river to reach a remote village on a mission of mercy and service to extend support and help to the village imam and his congregation. The imam turned out to be a pious elder who could barely read and write, and he had completely confused the cycles of the daily prayer. Even worse, his recitation of the sura *Al-Fatiha* (the most important chapter of the Qur'an) was terribly botched. The visitors spent an entire week painstakingly teaching him essential verses of the Qur'an and the cycles of prayer. On the return trip, as the teacher and his disciples were congratulating themselves (and thanking God) that they had been able to rescue the village in the nick of time, a voice rang out across the waters:

"Forgive me, but I've forgotten how to pronounce some of the words of the *Fatiha*." To his utter astonishment, the religious scholar saw the village elder running on the waters toward him. Humbled and chastened, the wide-eyed scholar had the wisdom to shout, "Don't worry about pronunciation! Just continue saying the words in your own sincere way!"

Truthfulness

Closely related to sincerity is the divine quality of truthfulness. We know this interrelationship in the sense of the expression, "Mean what you say and say what you mean." Our souls aspire to speak and live the truth, and that is not surprising because one of the beautiful names of Allah is *Al-Haq*, meaning the Truth. "A goodly word," says the Qur'an, referring not only to the divine message but also to the truthful words of believers, "is like a good tree, firmly rooted, reaching its branches toward the sky, always yielding fruit, by consent of its Sustainer" (14:24). An untruthful word, by contrast, "is that of an evil tree: It is torn up by the root from the surface of the Earth: It has no stability" (14:26). Be then, says the Qur'an, "ever steadfast in ... bearing witness to the truth for the sake of God, even though it be against your own selves" (4:135). The extent to which we can fulfill this injunction depends, of course, on our relationship with our ego. Very often our ego lapses into "truth of convenience." We go to great lengths to justify our partial truths and our tepid actions in upholding truth. Living the truth at every moment is very inconvenient.

A great danger when we are aspiring to be truthful but have not yet tamed the ego is to fall into the "truth trap." We become self-righteous about our purity and we love to tell the truth when it satisfies our need for self-glory. A story was told to me numerous times (evidently I needed to hear it!) about the thirteenth-century sage Saadi of Shiraz, who wrote in his classic book *Gulistan* about how, as a small child, he kept vigil all night long and prayed with his devout father. One night during the vigil, he noticed that others around him had succumbed to sleep. Turning to his father, he proudly proclaimed the truth. "Not one of them lifts up his head to perform a prayer. They are so profoundly asleep that you would say they are dead." His father tenderly replied, "My son, my life! It would be better if you too were asleep rather than backbiting other people."

There is a difficult ethical issue regarding truthfulness that all spiritual seekers struggle to resolve. Are we morally bound to tell the truth under all circumstances, even if it means putting a life in danger? Islam answers this question by permitting *taqiyya,* meaning "dissimulation," to protect life under certain circumstances. Though the Qur'an does not mention the word *taqiyya,* it does seem to validate the practice when it says "except under compulsion" in its condemnation of those who deny their religion (16:106). If you would be killed for professing your faith, the Qur'an seems to say you may conceal the truth. The topic of *taqiyya* often comes up during the question-and-answer period when I speak about Islam, and some people criticize Islam because it permits the practice, albeit under very limited circumstances. Before I could answer that reproach from a fundamentalist Christian on one such occasion, a young Jew leapt to his feet and asked the accuser, "Let's say you were a Christian living in Germany at the time of Hitler and you, as an upright follower of Jesus, secretly gave me refuge in your house. Suppose a Nazi soldier knocked on your door and asked you if you were harboring any Jews in your house. Would you say, 'Yes'? Or would you find it morally acceptable in your heart to say, 'No'?" How would you answer that question? In Islamic spirituality, whether dissimulation is permitted depends entirely on the truthfulness and sincerity of your intention.

꿏

REFLECTIONS
AND
PRACTICE

Select one of God's "beautiful names" (pages 225–228) and say it to your heart over and over again. For example, to cultivate patience you might repeat the divine name *Ya Sabur*, meaning O Patient One, as often as you can remember. Address the Heart within your heart, thereby cultivating a direct connection with the Beloved. Over time, as you persistently dip your heart in the vat of divine patience, you will find that it has truly taken on that sacred dye. If the dye you want is truthfulness, chant the name *Ya Haq*, O Truthful One.

✦ To deepen the quality of sincerity, continuously ask yourself, "Do my words match my intentions? Do my actions reflect my belief?" Dip your heart in the vat of sacred sincerity and remind yourself of the promise to the "sincere servants of God": "For them is a sustenance determined ... and they shall enjoy honor and dignity in gardens of felicity" (37:41–43).

✦ When moved to "speak your truth," ask yourself (1) whether it is kind and necessary, and (2) whether you are speaking from the little self of ego or the higher self of compassion and justice.

✦ In the same notebook where you note your ego qualities, also record the divine qualities that you have observed each day. Express deep gratitude to the Source and pray for these qualities to grow and flourish in your heart.

"Embrace Not Only the Ten Thousand Joys of Life, But Also the Ten Thousand Sorrows"

(TRADITIONAL SAYING)

IN THE SACRED WORK OF REMOVING VEILS BETWEEN human heart and divine Heart, it is critical to give ourselves permission to experience our feelings fully. By honoring all our feelings, our heart opens up more expansively to the Light. In the metaphor of Rumi, a mysterious window opens up from heart to Heart.

The radiance of the Moon fills the sky, says Rumi, but how can we enjoy it if the window of our heart is closed? Sadly, our natural inclination is to protect our tender hearts from the trials and tribulations of life, so we keep the windows of our hearts closed and shuttered, even though that means the delight of life's good fortune can't really touch us, either. In this state of sensory deprivation, we end up living lives of listlessness, apathy, and boredom. This is why Sufi teachers advise us to open up those windows and embrace whatever joys and sorrows come streaming through. When we allow ourselves to enfold not only our joys but also our sorrows, the windows of our heart open up more fully.

The Qur'an says that it is God who gave us feelings, and therefore it is important to honor all feelings (23:78 and 53:43). We tend to avoid and deny difficult feelings, such as anger and pain, that arise from our trials and tribulations. But remember that all our feelings, even the most negative, are just energies begging to be acknowledged, embraced, and integrated into the whole of who we are. If we ignore them and try to push them away, they will return again and again to haunt us. If we try to prevent them by hiding our hearts behind stone walls of denial, isolation and withdrawal, we paradoxically increase their intensity. Imagine that feelings in the heart are like salt in water. If we pour a boxful of salt into a glass of water, the result is bitter and unpalatable. But if we pour the same amount of salt into a pond or a lake, the effect is virtually unnoticeable. Similarly, if our hearts are clenched and small, the difficult feelings are intolerable, but if they are open and spacious, we scarcely notice the bitterness. Also, there is now so much more space for love, joy, and passion to flow into.

Sacred Trembling

Have you not noticed, says Rumi, that fruits never grow on the trunks of trees? They are always perched on branches, because to receive the blush of the Beloved, they have to quiver and tremble in the breeze.

The Sufi elder of a village in my native Bangladesh once told me that one of the reasons God gave us a human body is that the body makes us aware of what needs our attention and love on the spiritual plane. By greeting our physical sensations with awareness and compassion, we move closer to the divine Heart. The students of this elder met daily in a mango grove to practice a variation of Sacred Trembling, and villagers were often astonished to see the students' expressions of vulnerability as their feelings were reflected in their faces, postures, and breathing. Rather than being merely curious about the strange sight of these trembling students, the villagers instinctively felt that they were witnessing something sacred and transformative.

In fact, Islamic spirituality holds that the transformation wrought through physical experience of our feelings is so beautiful and powerful that even angels are jealous and in awe of our abilities. And no wonder: Our sages tell us that when we receive the sensations with awareness and work with compassion to transform our being, we have the potential to rise higher than the angels.

The poet Rumi coined many metaphors to convince us to do the work of honoring our difficult feelings. In one, the heart is like a guesthouse where some of the guests are unruly and trash the place. But these unpleasant guests may also be clearing the way for some new delight or joy in our life. Rumi asks us to greet the "dark thought," the "shame," the "malice" at the door with laughter and invite them in, for they have been "sent as a guide from beyond." As we work through our difficult feelings, sometimes we gain fresh insights that pave the way for unexpected blessings.

Sometimes we shut ourselves off from our difficult feelings in an effort to avoid or deny them. Rumi describes these dreaded feelings as energy sensations that are shouting, "Stop! Pay attention! Dig here!" If we have the courage to take a pickax and break open our stony hearts, we will be amazed to find that "the heart's matrix is glutted with rubies" and springs of laughter are buried within. If the heart opens and streams of tears pour out, know that these waters are holy. Wherever water falls, life flourishes; wherever tears fall, divine mercy is shown. Nature also celebrates our teardrops, Rumi says: The bough is made green and fresh by the weeping cloud and the candle is made brighter by its weeping.

As we move through the process of honoring our difficult feelings, it is critical to reiterate an axiom from the spiritual traditions: "Don't run toward pain and suffering; just don't run away from them." The encounter with our difficult feelings is like going through a deep and dark forest: Half the time we are going in, but the other half we are coming out. Once you begin, don't turn back. Eventually, the path will lead to a landscape of spaciousness and hope.

Joy Talk

As important as it is to embrace our difficult feelings, it is also important not to wallow in them. Rumi counsels that sometimes we have to tell our sadness, "Enough is enough!" Unremitting sadness is a blasphemy against the Hand of Splendor granting us joy and hope. Why do we choose to remain stuck in our prison cell when the door has swung open to a rose garden, and a mystery of light is melting the iron barriers of the windows? There comes a time when we need to speak of "roses and pomegranates," Rumi says, and join the "joy talk" of trees murmuring among themselves and nightingales sipping the nectar of sweet young fruits.

REFLECTIONS
AND
PRACTICE

During a typical day, how do you deal with difficult feelings? Do you tend to avoid or deny them?

+ To sanctify our painful feelings, perform this beautiful spiritual practice to allow yourself to tremble with your feelings in the process of Sacred Holding. Here's how: Allow yourself to experience a difficult feeling, locate that feeling in your body and, little by little, with compassion for yourself, allow your being to "tremble" with that feeling as you breathe through the physical holding. With time and practice, you will discover that painful feelings are replaced by sensations of sacredness and mercy, and your heart is increasingly open to holy joy.

+ Spend some time doing a sacred writing exercise. Write down all the feelings and thoughts associated with a difficult situation or emotional state. Then be silent for a while and touch your heart to get in touch with your higher self. When you are ready, write a response to yourself, beginning with the words, "Dear one, this is your Beloved speaking. I have heard your sighs and read your notes, and I want to tell you ..." Finish the letter on a note of mercy and compassion, allowing your higher self to speak freely to your wounded heart.

"There Is Room Inside for Only One of Us"

(RUMI)

IN THE *MASNAVI-L MA'NAVI* (*RHYMING COUPLETS OF Profound Spiritual Meaning*), Rumi tells a delightful story about a lover who is seized with longing to see his beloved and knocks on her door. "Who is it?" she asks, and he naturally responds, "It's me." The beloved is silent for a moment and then, in a voice aching with sadness, she replies, "Alas, there is room inside for only one of us." She declines to open the door and the lover, hurt and confused, turns away. He wanders the world for many years, seeking answers to his heart's desire. Finally, having grown in experience, wisdom, and higher knowledge, he returns to the door of his beloved and knocks. "Who is it?" she asks again, and this time the lover replies, "It's you!" Joyously, the beloved flings open the door and cries out, "Come in! There is room for both of us!" At that, lover and beloved melt into each other's embrace.

Just as that lover discovered, we too know that we cannot truly give our hearts to the Beloved if we are still attached to our own ego. "God has not made for any man two hearts in his [one] body" (33:4), says the Qur'an. So while we may speak metaphorically about divine

Heart in human heart, in reality we have but one human heart and our task is to decide whether we will honor the heart's deeper longing for connection to Spirit or settle for superficial understandings to satisfy the devices and desires of the ego. Spiritual teachers caution us to reflect on the course of our life before giving a pat answer. We may utter beautiful words about how our religion enjoins us to devote ourselves to God, but do we live our beliefs?

The Meaning of *Islam*

The word *Islam* refers both to the religion of Muslims and to the universal path of self-surrender to God. The latter is about the inner work that is the unifying theme of this book: giving up attachment to the little self in exchange for union with the higher self, saying, "It's *You,* God" rather than insisting, "It's all about me." By any other name, the path of surrender is an integral part of every religion, but it is also a path we tend to avoid. Such avoidance is detrimental, according to the Qur'an:

> We believe in Allah, and in what has been revealed to us and what was revealed to Abraham, Ismail, Isaac, Jacob, and the Tribes, and in [the Books] given to Moses, Jesus, and the prophets from their Lord: We make no distinction between one and another among them, and to Allah do we bow our will [in Islam]. If anyone desires a religion other than Islam [submission to Allah], never will it be accepted of him; and in the hereafter he will be in the ranks of those who have lost [all spiritual good]. (3:84–85)

It is crucial to understand that this passage is not about the superiority of a religion called Islam, as many mistakenly assume. Rather, it is about the path toward union with the Source and Sustainer of all that is, as prophets and sages have taught since ancient times. The word *submission* might better be rendered *surrender,* and Sufi masters teach that the true meaning of these verses is that mere mental investment in religious beliefs is ineffective if we eschew the work of self-surrender to divine Heart. We may spout any creed we want, but if we don't do the inner work, we are, in Rumi's words, "all husk and no kernel." We are among those who will lose in the hereafter, just as the Mulla keeps losing during the weekly lottery because he fails to do the necessary work. "O my Sustainer," he pleads, "life is hard and I really need the money. Please, O please, let me win the lottery." Finally the Sustainer speaks to the Mulla in a vision: "O Mulla, be at peace. You shall win the lottery! But do Me a favor. Be not so lazy and stingy. Take the step of buying at least one ticket!"

The surrender that we are talking about is not a craven submission to some demanding God in the sky; it is a deep honoring of our True Self. It is the soul's dynamic and co-creative role in the will of God, giving up limited will to participate in cosmic will. When you set in the west, says Rumi, your light rises from the east. The ascendance of the human to God becomes the descendance of God to the human. A popular hadith promises, "Whoever belongs to God, God belongs to him."

Where Will You Find a Customer Like God?

What stands in the way of our surrender? The fourteenth-century Sufi poet Hafiz summarizes our dilemma: God is trying to sell us something, but we refuse to buy. This refusal to purchase is our suffering. Unconsciously, we engage in what Hafiz calls "fantastic haggling" and "manic screaming over the price." Unable to understand the supreme benefits of this divine exchange, we cling tightly to our ego's desires and possessions. "If one desires the rewards of this world, let him remember that with God are the rewards of both this world and the life to come" (4:134), and "In the bounty of Allah and in His Mercy—in that let them rejoice: that is better than the [wealth] they hoard" (10:58). Where will we ever find a customer like God, Rumi asks. The All-Gracious One accepts our counterfeit coins and repays us in gold. "Sell and buy at once!" Continuing in this vein, Rumi rhapsodizes about the divine exchange: For a little earthly rose that we let go of, we receive hundreds of rose gardens in return; for one weak breath, the divine Breath!

REFLECTIONS

✦ Recall the primordial covenant between God and humanity (*Alastu bi Rabbikum*) described in Gem 3 and contemplate the Islamic belief that our work in this lifetime is to bring that cosmic state of surrender into consciousness and live it day by day here on Earth.

What prevents you from surrendering your ego to God? What is one simple step you can take right now to move you forward on the path of surrender?

✦ The concept is simple, but not always easy. The nineteenth-century Hindu saint Ramakrishna said that God's grace is like a breeze. It is always flowing and is present in the beginning, middle, and end of our lives. But we need to raise the sail to catch the wind. Sailors know that raising the sail can be hard work, especially in heavy seas. But without making the effort, we are at the mercy of the elements.

What changes can you make to effect a shift from the ego's need to please others to the soul's need to please God?

PRACTICE

✦ As often as you can remember, ask yourself, "In my speech and actions am I coming from a place of surrender to divine attributes (that is, love, compassion, truth, beauty) or am I coming from a place of the little self (fear, anger, pettiness, jealousy)?" Be mindful of the question and make conscious efforts to come from your God-surrendered soul.

✦ Take a few moments at bedtime to review your actions and motivations of the day. Have they been in accordance with your commitment to surrender ego-self to higher self? If yes, breathe a prayer of gratitude to the divine Breath within the breath. If not, spend a few minutes chanting *"Estaghfirullah"* (Gem 12) and re-solve, with compassion for self, to live more consciously tomorrow.

REMEMBERING
YOUR
SUSTAINER

"Bow in Adoration and Draw Closer"

(QUR'AN 96:19)

OF ALL THE MYRIAD WAYS WE HUMANS EXPRESS SURREN-
der to Divinity, perhaps the most basic one is to fall on our knees
in praise and adoration. Several times a day Muslims perform a
prayer ritual that combines Qur'anic verses, words of praise, and
body prayer. This ritual, some scholars say, was conceived during the mystical night journey of the Prophet Muhammad, who
was transported on a magical steed from Mecca to a rocky hilltop
in Jerusalem, the seat of earlier revelations to the first People of
the Book (17:1). As described in several hadith, Muhammad was
greeted there by the souls of many prophets and then, accompanied by the angel Gabriel, he ascended vertically through seven
levels of Heaven, finally arriving at the farthest boundary marked
by a lote tree "shrouded in mystery unspeakable" (53:16). Commentators suggest that Muhammad had reached the furthest
extent of knowledge that humans and angels can attain. There
the Prophet's sight "neither swerved nor wavered" (53:17) and in
the rapture of the moment "truly did he see signs of his Lord, the
Greatest" (53:18).

One of those signs was the vision of angels bowing and prostrating themselves to God while murmuring prayers of praise and gratitude. From this Muhammad concluded that we humans should use both body and soul in our prayers, and the Qur'an would seem to concur: "Bow down in adoration and draw closer" (96:19), says the Holy Book. Thus Islamic prayers consist of cycles of standing, bowing, prostrating, and sitting in sweet surrender to God while reciting verses of the Qur'an that express praise and thanksgiving. At the conclusion of the ritual prayers, Muslims turn their heads to the right and the left, murmuring words of praise and greetings to the angels who, it is said, rush into places of sacred worship. Jewish readers will recognize this practice as a form of their beautiful song "*Shalom Aleychem*" with which they greet the "Angels of the Exalted One" when they gather to welcome the Sabbath.

The Cycle of Prayer

How did Muhammad arrive at five as the required number of prayer cycles per day? Legend has it that the number emerged from a conversation he had with the prophet Moses, whom he met on his descent from the seventh level of Heaven. Moses asked, "How many times a day did God tell you Muslims to pray?" When Muhammad responded, "Fifty," Moses exclaimed, "They will never pray that often! Go back up and ask for a lesser number." After several bargaining trips back and forth from the mysterious realms to where Moses was waiting to hear the upshot, Muhammad told Moses that he bargained the number down to five times a day and was too shy to continue entreating God. Thus, Muslims perform five obligatory cycles of prayers each day. Sunni Muslims customarily pray five times a day, whereas Shia Muslims complete the five cycles in three prayer sessions.

The first prayer cycle of the day occurs before sunrise, and Rumi urges us not to sleep through it. He exhorts us to forget our life and say, "God is great!" He asks us to get up and ponder the question, "You think you know what time it is? It is time to pray!" The Qur'an extols the beauty of praying in the "small watches of the night" when "impressions are strongest and words are most eloquent" (73:6). Mystics believe the veils between visible and invisible worlds are like gossamer in the wee hours. In Rumi's beautiful imagery, it is as if "a dawn breeze has blown away the veil from the Face of God."

Perhaps the most special prayer cycle of the week is the one performed in community on Friday, which in Arabic is called *jummah*, which means "gathering." This is when Muslims congregate at the local mosque to perform a special cycle of midday prayers and listen to a sermon. According to a hadith qudsi, angels throng the mosque and bless the worshipers during this auspicious time. In the Qur'an, Allah says, "Remember Me, and I shall remember you" (2:152). In a number of hadith, God says that He remembers us better when we pray in community.

Call to Prayer and Ablution

A prayer cycle is preceded by the *Azan,* or call to prayer, typically sung by a muezzin in the mosque. "*Allahu akbar!*" ("God is great!"), shouts the caller. "Come to prayer for your own betterment!" The poet Kabir playfully asks why the muezzin has to proclaim the greatness of Allah so loudly and repeatedly. Surely the Creator, who easily hears the "anklets on the feet of insects" does not need the shouts of a muezzin extolling the grandeur of God! But, of course, Kabir knew these frequent calls are not meant for God. They are necessary reminders for us humans, who are easily distracted by the needs and desires of our material lives. To be in a state of mindfulness and purification before they stand in the presence of God, devotees perform ablutions with water to cleanse hands, arms, mouth, face, ears, nostrils, the nape of the neck, and feet while murmuring an inner prayer for guidance and mercy.

Humility and Presence

All these words about the ritual aspects of Islamic prayer notwithstanding, it is the sincerity of "drawing closer," not the etiquette of "bowing down," that is the most important element of prayer. The Prophet once asked his companions, "Why is it that I do not see sweetness in your worship?"[1] When asked what he meant, the Prophet replied, "Humility." Of what use are ritual words and postures if the prayer is not imbued with the glow of humble longing? Muhammad could well be a model for our approach to prayer: His companions noted that often when he prayed, the throbbing sobs within his breast sounded like a boiling pot.

Another model might be the simple shepherd in a celebrated story by Rumi. Rapt in communion with God, the shepherd spoke of his yearning to touch God's face, kiss His hands, comb His hair, and feed Him milk. The prophet Moses overheard the shepherd and began to chide him for blasphemous familiarity: "It sounds as if you're chatting with your uncles." One should not insult the Supreme Creator by naive babble, he said, whereupon the shepherd sighed repentantly. Later that night, God reproached Moses: "You have separated me from one of my own. Did you come as a prophet to unite or to sever?" It is not Divinity that is glorified in acts of worship, God reminded Moses, it is the worshiper! Forget the insistence on correct phraseology. God looks inside the humility. That broken-open lowliness is the reality, not the language.

The shepherd in Rumi's tale is also a beautiful model of presence or mindfulness in communion with God. "No prayer is complete without presence," said Muhammad, and in another hadith he advised, "Worship God as if you see Him and if you cannot see Him, know that He sees you." The simple shepherd was seeing God with the eyes of his loving heart, and God clearly saw the shepherd and knew him as "one of my own." The need for mindfulness in the presence of Supreme Majesty is illustrated by a story about the seventeenth-century Mughul emperor Akbar, who was bowing and prostrating himself to God in the stillness of a forest in India. Out of nowhere, a young peasant girl, distressed with thoughts of her missing husband, almost tripped over the emperor, totally oblivious of the devotee in prayer. The emperor was furious. "How dare you cross my prayer path? Have you no respect for someone in prayer?" Trembling with fear, the girl explained that she hadn't seen the emperor because she had been lost in thoughts of her beloved husband. Then, daring to look at him, she wondered how he had been able to see her if he had been lost in adoration of his Beloved! Rightly feeling chastened, the emperor released the girl and gave her a handsome reward for teaching him a powerful lesson.

Praise and Gratitude

Islamic body prayer focuses on prayers of praise and gratitude. The mystics say that when we praise God, we are creating feathers and wings for the bird of Spirit within us. This insight is derived from a story in the Qur'an in which Jesus poured his breath on a bird of clay and magically the bird stirred to life "by Allah's leave" (3:49). With our prayers of praise and gratitude, we come into alignment with a universal vibration. "Are you not aware that it is God whose limitless glory all creatures in the Heavens and on Earth praise, even the birds as they outspread their wings?" (24:41).

When we are grateful even in times of affliction, we are giving thanks for unknown blessings already on their way. The Mulla was aware of this mysterious secret when his donkey disappeared. The entire village turned out to help him look for it, but to no avail. The donkey was lost forever. At sunset they came to give the Mulla the bad news and found him on his knees in the town square, praising and thanking God. The puzzled villagers, thinking that he must have misunderstood their arrival, repeated that the donkey was lost for good. "I know! I know!" he exclaimed. "I am just so grateful to God because imagine what could have happened to me if I had been on the donkey!"

A beautiful monthlong prayer of gratitude is the practice of fasting in the month of Ramadan, the ninth month of the Islamic lunar calendar. It was in this month that the Night of Power occurred, and the first verses of the Qur'an were revealed to the Prophet and, through him, to all humanity. In gratitude, Muslims fast during the daylight hours because, as Rumi says, our bodies are like lutes and if our sound box is stuffed, we are unable to hear the music of our souls singing, "Allah! Allah!"

A favorite traditional Sufi prayer of gratitude is as follows: "O God, favor upon favor have you bestowed upon this handful of dust. Thank you."

Supplication and Increased Necessity

There is also time during prostrations to make our supplications known to the Giver of all gifts. God tells us in the Qur'an, "I listen to the prayer of every supplicant" (2:186). But He goes on to say that humans tend to be "hasty" and many of their prayers are not in their highest interest (17:11). Sufi teachers advise that when making supplications to God, we should express our needs humbly, mindfully, and with "increased necessity" from the depths of our souls. Have you not noticed, asks Rumi, that when a child is born, the mother's breasts become filled with milk? When there is an increased need, the Universe provides. Never one to wait passively for divine blessings, Rumi once prayed to God that he would continue to cry out from the depths of his soul with fervor and intensity, "until the milk of Thy loving-kindness boils over!"

My grandfather, known as a "rainmaker" as well as a Sufi teacher and healer, took Rumi's words to heart. Village elders and officials in northern Bengal often enlisted his help to pray for rain in areas of drought. Before physically going to the parched area, he would spend several days in intense prayer and meditation, praising and thanking God with utmost sincerity and begging God to bless the village with rain. On the appointed day he would walk the parched lands with arms outstretched and palms cupped to receive the desired blessing. From the innermost core of his being, he repeatedly cried out to God for rain. Sometimes, in spite of his prolonged pleas, nothing happened. At other times, he felt an inner "click," confirming a mysterious connection, and very soon after that the Heavens opened and the rain came down in torrents.

Blessings and Benefits

Our prayers of supplication are all received by our Creator and God answers them in a mysterious and timely way. Why do we need to prostrate ourselves to God in praise and gratitude? God surely doesn't need them. The truth is it is we who benefit in at least three major ways. The first is aptly summarized in a traditional saying: "One prostration of prayer to God frees you from a thousand prostrations to your ego." The second is the growth of intimacy between adorer and the Beloved. Dr. Ann Holmes Redding, a scholar of the Christian scriptures and for twenty-five years an Episcopal priest, was so moved by her experience of the Islamic body prayer that she adopted Islam as her personal religion alongside her life-long Christianity. Ann reports that when surrendering to God in body prayer, she experiences a deep inner calm and an exquisite closeness to God. Every prayer session, she says, is "a divine date with God."

The third major benefit of body prayer is that it opens the eyes of the heart to perceive creative and sacred opportunities in our lives. Consider the story of the Mulla, who was unjustly imprisoned and was counting on his beloved teacher to smuggle in a key or other means of escape when he came to visit. In due course, the teacher arrived, gave the Mulla a prayer rug, and told him to pray regularly. What a letdown! But the Mulla, having time on his hands, reluctantly began doing the daily cycles of body prayer on the new rug. And as he bowed and prostrated himself on the rug, he began to notice that it had a special design. Slowly it dawned on him: The design incorporated an escape route from the prison!

REFLECTIONS

In a hadith reported by Ayesha, during good times the Prophet used to say, "Praise be to God, whose grace brings all goodness to perfection," and in difficult times he said, "Praise be to God under all conditions."

Can you create a personal prayer of gratitude to use regularly?

PRACTICE

+ All of us, no matter what our religion, can create a personal daily prayer routine. Choose a regular time each day—perhaps when you rise in the morning or just before you retire at night. Choose a style of prayer that feels authentic to you. What matters is not so much the words you say (whether they are your own or from a prayer book), but the love and sincerity in your heart.

+ To make prayer a more routine part of your day, consider setting an alarm on your watch or computer and spending even just a few moments in mental but heartfelt prostration and acknowledgment of Divinity.

+ Rumi said, "Like the angels, make the glorification of God your sustenance." Develop the habit of glorifying and thanking God as often as you can throughout the day. You will feel "shifts," and experience blessings in your inner and outer world.

"Truly in the Remembrance of God Do Hearts Find Rest"

(QUR'AN 13:28)

THE PROPHET MUHAMMAD RELATED THAT MOSES ONCE asked God if he should address Him loudly or in a whisper. That is, is God physically distant or nearby? God replied, "O Moses! I am the Companion of My servant when he remembers Me." "Truly," says the Qur'an, "in the remembrance of God do hearts find rest."

The continual remembrance of God is a fundamental goal of many spiritual traditions, and metaphors abound for the beauty and necessity of such a practice. We humans, separated from our Source, are like fish thrashing around and quivering when plucked from life-sustaining waters. The fish feel no spiritual joy without the sea. Visiting the sea only a few times a week will not suffice! Just so, praying at intervals—no matter how regular—will not keep us immersed in the living waters of divine compassion and mercy. Thus the Holy Book urges us to cultivate a constant sense of God's presence by remaining "steadfast in prayer" so that we don't lapse into impatience and discouragement at life's vicissitudes throughout the day (70:19–23).

To those who remain conscious of God, says the Qur'an, God provides in ways we could never imagine (65:3)—or, as Rumi did imagine it, God sends "a stretcher from Grace" whenever we need it. The Qur'an waxes poetic about the blessings of God-consciousness: We will receive divine light, guidance, forgiveness, and abundant mercy, and—best of all—"Paradise will be brought near to the God-conscious, no longer will it be distant" (50:31). For his part, Rumi also waxes poetic, declaring to the Beloved that the beauties of Earth give him much joy and pleasure, but "if You are not with me, these do not matter. And if You are with me, these do not matter!"

So how can we cultivate a continual remembrance of God in the midst of our busy lives? A common practice is to choose a sacred word or verse and repeat it as often as possible during the course of the day: while commuting, while waiting for the elevator, while standing in line at the coffee shop. A favorite verse for Muslims is the statement, *La ila ha il Allah*. Literally meaning "There is no God but God," it also implies there is no reality aside from God, since God is the Source and Essence of all that is. This is the phrase Muhammad recommended when his son-in-law, Hazrat Ali, asked what was the shortest way to Allah's presence. "But give me something special," pleaded Ali. The Prophet replied that if all the Heavens and Earth were placed on one side of a scale and *La ila ha il Allah* were placed on the other, the latter would be heavier. Another mantra, based on another set of prayers recommended by the Prophet, is *Subhan Allah, Al-hamdulillah, Allahu Akbar* (Glory be to God, Praise be to God, God is Great).

Meadows of Paradise

"If you find the meadows of Paradise," said the Prophet, "linger there." Muhammad was referring to gatherings of devotees for the sole purpose of remembering God. This is a practice known as *zikr* ("remembrance" in Arabic) and Sufis have perfected the art of gathering in circles to collectively recite and chant sacred words and verses. Sessions sometimes last all night and devotees talk of a presence that envelops the circle, producing a sweetness that Rumi says "existed before honey or bee." Drawing on the mystical sense of gossamer veils between visible and invisible worlds, Rumi exults, "When the night sky pours by, it is really a crowd of beggars and they are begging for just this." In some *zikr* circles, devotees sit quietly, deep in silent remembrance of God. The beauty and joy of a silent communion with God is beyond words.

REFLECTIONS

Keep your tongue forever moistened with the name of Allah.   HADITH

Call upon your Sustainer humbly and in the secrecy of your hearts.   QUR'AN 7:55

Can you think of a sacred word or sentence that, when re-peated in the heart, evokes for you a unique connection with Mystery?

PRACTICE

The following Sufi exercise is based on a practice of the Prophet Muhammad, who, before passing through the door of a mosque, always offered a prayer, "O Allah! Open for me the doors of Your Mercy!" In this exercise we are asked to transform any routine activity in our life into a sacred and metaphorical prayer. This might bring astonishing beauty and meaning into our everyday lives. For example, when showering, the prayer might be, "O God, may these waters cleanse my impurities and renew my spirit." When dressing, "May this covering be a mantle of divine protection." When undressing we might say, "As I remove my clothing, I am peeling off layers of my ego."

DOING
WHAT IS
BEAUTIFUL

"Persevere in Doing Good: Behold! God Loves the Doers of Good."

(QUR'AN 2:195)

THE QUR'AN SAYS THAT OUR WORSHIP IS INCOMPLETE IF we do not extend it in service to God's creatures great and small. True righteousness is not merely turning our faces toward east or west, says the Qur'an; rather, it is to believe God's messages sent through the prophets and to spend of our substance, out of love for God, "for your kin, for orphans, for the needy, for the wayfarer, for those who ask, and for the ransom of slaves." It is, furthermore, to be steadfast in prayer and to practice regular charity; to fulfill the contracts we have made; and to be firm and patient in pain and adversity. Quite a tall order—and all in one Qur'anic verse (2:177)—but a beautiful way to live! So, "persevere in doing good: Behold! God loves the doers of good."

As if to reinforce the idea of service as a form of worship, Shams of Tabriz (the teacher whose spiritual knowledge so transformed Rumi) offers the image of Muslims all around the world bowing and prostrating themselves in the direction of the Kabah, the symbolic House of God in Mecca. What happens if you remove the Kabah?

Look! The worshipers are bowing to one another! This is the true maturation of our search for the Beloved: the ability to see God's presence in every soul we meet. Expanding on the countless opportunities we have to worship God by doing what is beautiful for one another, Rumi says that we must express the beauty we love in what we do, for "there are hundreds of ways to kneel and kiss the ground."

Three Qur'anic Guidelines

What makes our acts of service good? The Holy Book has three specific suggestions about the best kinds of service for those "who seek the countenance of God" (30:38). First, "spend freely in the way of God" (47:38) and "give freely of what you love" (3:92) to those who ask and those who do not ask (2:177 and 70:25). Second, give quietly without fanfare. "God is well acquainted with what you do," says the Qur'an, and helping the needy without claiming credit will atone for some of our wrongdoings (2:271). The third and most beautiful kind of service is working to bring about structural and systemic changes in society for the common good.

There is a passionate passage in the Qur'an about this third kind of service. In it, God laments that too few of us are inclined to climb the "path that is steep," the path that is essentially about "freeing a slave from bondage" and reaching out to "the indigent down in the dust," even though we have been given eyes to see injustice and lips to speak out against it (90:11–16). Fearing inconvenience or perhaps some real danger to ourselves if we get involved, we turn a blind eye and seal our lips. We could learn from the beautiful example of Yasmin. She is working to improve the lot of desperately poor village children who pour into Dhaka (the capital city of Bangladesh) to work as servants. These children are often abused because of their vulnerability. Like many upper-class Bengalis, she herself employs domestic servants, some of them as young as nine years old, but none is abused and all are treated with dignity and care. Realizing that her personal kindness does little to undo the basic evil of child servitude, Yasmin seizes every opportunity to speak in public forums about exploitation of children. Not only does she speak out, but she alsodoes something remarkably practical to help these children: She has set up a free school in her large house to teach reading, writing, math, and music to the young servants in her neighborhood. She recruited family, friends, teachers, and students to volunteer their time and talents, and she went door to door begging homeowners to release their young servants for two to three hours every day during the afternoon siesta. Collaboratively, Yasmin and her volunteers are working to free these children from the yoke of illiteracy that dooms them to a life of hopelessness and exploitation.

Closer to home, in our Interfaith Community Sanctuary in Seattle, there are dedicated people who are committed to obtaining help and treatment for servicemen and -women who have been unable to return to "normal" civilian life because of their physical injuries and post-traumatic stress. Others work diligently in the cause of humane treatment of the animals we eat and responsible methods of growing and transporting the food on our table. Some have worked to "follow the money" and share their findings so that the rest of us can make conscientious choices about spending and investing where it will do the most good. All who engage in such system-altering activities are "companions of the Right Hand [that is, doers of righteousness]" (90:18), says the Qur'an. They are the ones who have chosen to climb the steep path by truly walking the talk. We can take small steps alongside them by supporting their causes and listening to our own inner voices telling us how we can act responsibly and righteously in the service of Allah.

Righteous Deeds

Indeed, doing righteous deeds is a major theme in the Qur'an. It matters not what we have accumulated on this Earth in terms of wealth and power. When we die, these will be left behind. It is beautiful to count among our loved ones family members and close friends. But they can accompany us only up to the grave. Beyond that, it is the grace and power of righteous deeds that will carry us into the presence of God. It is our deeds of righteousness that are best in the sight of God and that bear eternal fruit (16:30).

To sustain our ability to serve others, it is critical that we also nurture and nourish ourselves. Thus the first act of service is to bring love and healing to ourselves, gently and mercifully healing our own suffering and dysfunction. When we heal our past wounds, we bring less anger, confusion, and pain into the world. We have more space inside us to hold the other's suffering with understanding, compassion, and mercy. We become peace bearers and peacemakers. We are able to practice the golden rule as enunciated by the Prophet: "No one of you can be a true believer unless he wishes for his brother what he wishes for himself."

The Prophet emphasized that many of our most beneficial acts of service to others do not involve wealth or power. Our most enduring gifts include a cheerful disposition, hospitality, and graciousness. One of the best parts of Islam, he explained, is to "extend greetings to all whom you know and whom you do not know." When you take the initiative and shake someone's hand with joy and sincerity, "a hundred mercies descend, ninety of them for the one who began the handshake." One of the best actions in life, explained the Prophet, is to "gladden the heart of another." Our good nature is a gift to the world. But the virtue of graciousness is not just about giving aid and being cheerful, said the Prophet. It is also about self-restraint in the face of insult or defamation. "If a man defames you with what he knows about you, do not defame him with what you know about him. For the sin is against him." Rumi seconds that advice: "Veil the faults of others so that yours might be veiled."

In Islam there is one more service to be performed, the time-honored tradition of praying daily for the souls of our departed parents and doing occasional acts of charity in their name. The beauty of this tradition is exemplified by the story of a poor water carrier in the city of Samarqand, who pledged to give his Friday's earnings to the poor for the benefit of his parents' souls. He kept his promise for many years, until one Friday he had earned no money. What to do?

He consulted a spiritual teacher, who advised him to gather up the skins of melons and watermelons and feed them to hungry animals. This he did, and that night his father and mother appeared to him in a dream. "Allah bless you!" they cried out. "You used to send us a present every Friday, and now this Friday night, we received as a divine gift the melons and watermelons of Paradise!"

REFLECTIONS

> Do good deeds according to your capacity. God never tires of giving rewards unless you tire of doing good. The good deeds most loved by God are those that are done regularly, even if they are small.   HADITH

What actions do you perform regularly that qualify in your mind as good deeds?

PRACTICE

✦ Remember to make time for yourself, especially to hold your own pain and sadness with gentleness and mercy. Be of service to your own being. This expands your ability to be of service to others; it is a gift not only to yourself but also to divine Spirit and to the world.

✦ Make it a habit to engage every day in beautiful deeds, no matter how small they appear to be: a smile, a kind word, mindful presence, a short prayer, a helping hand, a small donation. These little acts are an important part of our sacred mission and we become, in the words of Rumi, a "lamp, lifeboat, or ladder" to God's creation.

"Ah! What a Beautiful Fellowship!"

(QUR'AN 4:69)

ONE OF THE GREATEST JOYS IN LIFE IS TO BE BLESSED with authentic community, an intimate circle of companions who love, nurture, support, and guide us. In the words of the ninth-century female teacher Umm Abdallah, "Being in the company of one's spiritual brethren is the consolation for being in the abode of materiality."[1] If we are fortunate to have such a collection of sincere, loving, and devoted family members and friends, we have been blessed with what Rumi calls a Circle of Love. As the Holy Book exclaims, "Ah! What a beautiful fellowship!"

The simple truth is that we need authentic community in our lives. It is not enough to choose friends just for fun and games—we also need friends who share our values and are there to support us with counsel and consolation in the hard times as well as the easy. As we ascend the steep path toward spiritual enlightenment, companions help ease the way and encourage us when we falter. Our friend Rumi expresses this eloquently with metaphors. A wall standing alone is useless, but together with other walls it can support a roof. Rushes and reeds left on their own may blow away in the wind, but when

126

woven together they may serve as a roof for shelter or a mat for rest. When wool meets with a gifted carpet maker, it becomes a miracle of rich design. Even the Prophet sought a Circle of Love. In his community he had many followers, but he also had an inner circle who were known as his companions. These were friends—both men and women—"who hearken to their Lord" and with whom he conducted spiritual affairs "by mutual consultation" (42:38).

We too are encouraged to consult our Circle of Love for creative solutions to seemingly unsolvable problems. Sufis tell the story about two men—one blind and one lame—who were invited to the king's banquet. Both were overjoyed until reality set in. Then the blind man lamented, "Alas, I can't see and the road is treacherous. How will I ever find my way?" while the lame man bemoaned, "What a tragedy! The way is long and my legs won't make it." But when their circle of friends heard about the problem, one of them came up with a solution: The lame man could piggyback on the blind man and use his eyes to guide the strong legs of his blind companion. In this manner they were both able to attend the king's banquet. This is how it is in life: We all carry pain and insecurities that can blind or disable us in other ways, but we can still get to the banquet. All we need is support and advice from our Circle of Love, and a willingness to collaborate.

Our need for such a circle becomes critical as we age. Our journey to the moment of death goes much more smoothly when we experience the support and affection of our Circle of Love. It is heartbreaking that some people end up suffering and dying alone. One incident in my early ministry is seared in my memory. A woman had come to a few of my services, and it seemed there was something she wanted to say, but she always slipped away as soon as the service was over. Finally, I managed to catch her before she left, and she very shyly introduced herself. She lived in the neighborhood and longed for some sense of community. With pain in her eyes, she asked if I could help. Before I could say anything, someone else greeted me warmly and I was momentarily distracted, and in that instant she was gone. She never returned, but I remembered her name. Many months later, I read in the local newspaper that she had been found dead in her home. Evidently, her body had been lying there for over two months, unnoticed and untended because her quest for community had presumably gone unfulfilled. I felt devastated and remorseful, but also more determined than ever to help create authentic community for everyone who seeks it, and especially for those who are lonely and isolated.

Three Gateways to Authentic Community

If authentic community is so necessary in life, then it is important to ask what kind of people should be invited into our Circle of Love. Sufi teachers point to three essentials—love, trust, and truth—and encourage us to ask ourselves three basic questions.

First, "Whom do I love and who loves me in return?" Mutual affection is paramount. The ninth-century Sufi teacher Bayazid Bistami advises us to ally ourselves with the beloved of God, people "whose hearts tremble with awe whenever God is mentioned" (8:2) because it is the nature of such people to hold us in their hearts.

Second, "Whom do I truly trust?" Without trust there is little possibility of being vulnerable, and without vulnerability there is no authentic relationship.

And third, "Who in my life is dedicated to loving and living the truth?" The Qur'an advises, "Let there arise ... a band of people inviting to all that is good, enjoining what is right, and forbidding what is wrong: They are the ones who attain felicity" (3:104).

Clearly, the gateways of love, trust, and truth are highly selective. In the course of life, we may develop several circles of friends, but precious few will qualify for our sacred Circle of Love. It is our right and our duty to choose carefully, because the quality and direction of our lives depend on the quality of our close companions. Do not despair if you don't yet have such a circle, and don't lament that it seems so hard to acquire one. Continue to deepen your own inner work, and your sincerity and persistence will create a radiance that is bound to attract the right companions in good time. Rumi advises that if we increase our yearning for community, it will happen. "Don't seek water," he says. "Increase your thirst and water will gush from above and below." Hafiz fully agrees. Once we dedicate our lives to loving and serving the Friend, he says, the Beloved "will send you one of his wild companions—like Hafiz."

Though it may take time to build a flesh-and-blood Circle of Love, there is a time-honored Sufi meditation in which you can invoke an inner circle populated by some of these "wild" and sacred companions. Using the criteria of love, trust, and truth, you can create an inner Circle of Love composed of members drawn from your own imagination. As described in the next section ("Practice"), draw on your magical inner circle to experience the love and healing offered by authentic community while you wait for your outer Circle of Love to manifest.

REFLECTIONS

Come out of the Circle of Time and enter the Circle of Love.

RUMI

Choose the company of someone who reminds you of God, and the awe of whom will move your heart, someone who will counsel you with the tongue of deeds, not words.

IBN KHAFIF[2]

A person's spiritual practice is only as good as that of his close friends; so consider well whom you befriend.

PROPHET MUHAMMAD

From the pool of family members, relatives, friends, and acquaintances, who would you choose to be members of your outer Circle of Love?

PRACTICE

Follow these steps to experience the healing power of an inner Circle of Love.

1. Close your eyes, focus on your nostrils, and be mindful of your breath as you inhale and exhale. Stay with this for about three minutes. Then, using your imagination, allow yourself to drift gently into a "sacred sanctuary," a place that is absolutely safe, beautiful, and filled with energies of healing and love. Endow it with enchantment and magical properties: You may fly if you wish, or dive to coral gardens in the sea, or simply rest and soak up the beauty and healing of this place.

2. Now, summon your inner Circle of Love: loved ones living or deceased, prophets and saints, historical figures, animals, trees—anyone or anything your heart desires. The only limitation is your belief system.

3. It is in the nature of these members to love you. They shower you with love and light. Some or all of them come up to you and hold you tenderly. Allow yourself to be cherished, nurtured, and nourished. Surrender into the love and compassion they hold for you.

4. When it is time to come into awareness, say good-bye to each member of your circle. Receive their thanks and blessings and come into awareness.

Ah! What a beautiful fellowship you have created for yourself!

"Be Just; This Is Closest to Being God-Conscious."

(QUR'AN 5:8)

ALL HUMANS ARE BORN ESSENTIALLY GOOD, SAYS THE Qur'an, but we are inclined to be forgetful of our better nature and its attendant obligations. Caught up in earthly cycles of acquisition and competition, we can be selfish and unjust, sometimes to an extreme degree. We forget that we are God's representatives on Earth and heirs of what the Holy Book calls the "Trust" (33:72). The Qur'an does not elaborate on the meaning of this "Trust," but most commentators believe it refers to the gifts of awareness and free will, along with the responsibility to use these gifts in the service of God's creation by manifesting the divine traits of compassion, forbearance, and justice.

Justice is a central theme in the Qur'an, and indeed, *Al-Adl* (meaning "The Just") and *Al-Muqsit* ("The Equitable One") are two of the ninety-nine names ascribed to Allah in the Islamic tradition. God is the epitome of justice, says the Qur'an: Allah "does not wrong anyone as much as an atom's weight" (4:40) or "as much as the groove on the pit of a date" (4:124). Those whose lives have been savaged by circumstances beyond their control may question that statement, but an intriguing tale in the Qur'an hints that events in our lives are part of a larger story.

The tale in the Qur'an (18:60–82) involves the prophet Moses and a mysterious being traditionally identified as *Khidr,* meaning "Green," whose knowledge is "fresh and green" because it comes directly from God. Moses wants to understand the mysterious ways of God, so he begs to accompany Khidr on one of his earthly missions. Khidr refuses because he knows Moses will not understand what is happening, but he relents when Moses swears he just wants to observe and promises not to question. So they proceed, and along the way Khidr damages a boat, kills a youth, and restores a broken wall for townspeople who have been unspeakably rude to them. Beside himself over the seeming arbitrariness in every instance, Moses breaks his promise of silence and reproaches Khidr for what he has done. (In a delightfully human moment, Khidr asks Moses, "Didn't I tell you that you wouldn't understand?") At the conclusion of the journey, Khidr reveals the hidden reasons for his inexplicable actions. The boat was the sole source of livelihood for "men in dire want," so he rendered it undesirable to a despotic king who was seizing ships by force. The youth's life was ended because of his "overweening wickedness and denial of all truth," which would have brought unbearable grief on his godly parents. The wall was repaired because there was a treasure hidden underneath it that belonged to two orphans, and Allah wanted to keep the treasure hidden until the children reached maturity. Each of these actions, says Khidr, was "an act of mercy from your Sustainer and I did not act by my own commands" (18:82). This story is a good illustration of the need to be wary of making judgments about events and circumstances in life without higher awareness.

So all-encompassing is justice that it defies definition, but spiritual teachers enumerate some essential qualities that enable us to be just. Besides higher awareness, we need courage, a sense of proportion and equity, and mercy.

Courage

Courage means having the inner strength to act on our truth and be just in the face of obstacles, fear, or personal disadvantage. As God's representatives on Earth, we are expected to manifest divine justice regardless of the personal cost or our preference. Even if it means going against ourselves, our loved ones, or those we fear to offend, we are called by our primordial trust to "stand out firmly for justice" (4:135). The Qur'an says that even if others hate us, we must not swerve from justice. "Be just," says the Holy Book. "This is closest to being God-conscious" (5:8).

Supporting the command to be just, regardless of outer circumstances, the Qur'an cautions us not to be swayed by the prejudices and pressures of our community or religious affiliation. It cites the case of a Muslim who brought a false accusation against a Jew and was supported loudly and aggressively by his tribe. As the Prophet was adjudicating the case, he received a revelation reminding him to be guided by Allah: "So be not [used] as an advocate by those who betray their trust" (4:105). After an impartial sifting of the facts, the Prophet ruled against the Muslim. This ruling cost the Prophet the support of the man's tribe at a time when his community was struggling, but he sustained the sacred Trust of God.

Proportion and Equity for All God's Creation

Prior to the advent of Islam, Arabian tribesmen used disproportionate force to avenge a wrong. The Holy Book quotes the Mosaic law of "an eye for an eye and a tooth for a tooth" to define proportionality, but adds immediately, "But if anyone remits the retaliation by way of charity, it is an act of atonement for himself" (5:45). "Mandated is the law of equality," says the Qur'an, but it quickly adds, "but fear Allah and know that Allah is with those who restrain themselves" (2:194). We are being asked to do what is right, to protect ourselves and not allow ourselves to be abused, but also to restrain ourselves from vengeful impulses. Our ultimate goal is to strive to forgive those who have wronged us. The Qur'an says, "... if one is patient in adversity and forgives—this, behold, is indeed something to set one's heart upon!" (42:43).

In the following story, the Prophet's conduct exemplifies the need to be humble and honest in giving everybody, including oneself, his or her equitable due. A man rudely grabbed the Prophet's cloak at a funeral, glared at him "in an ugly fashion," and said, "Aren't you going to pay me my due? By God, I never knew you of the tribe of *Abd al-Muttalib* to be late payers." Apparently, the man had lent money to the Prophet and the loan was due that day. The Prophet's companion, Umar, could hardly believe his ears. How could the man dare to speak to the Messenger of God in this aggressive manner? Umar's eyes "rolled like revolving celestial bodies" and he threatened to cut off the man's head. The Prophet intervened and, "smiling quietly with gentleness," he said, "Umar, both he and I were in need of something other than that from you; you should have told me to pay up properly, and him to behave better." The Prophet instructed Umar to give the man his due, and additionally give him a gift of dates as a bonus.[1]

"Equity" justice, like charity, begins at home. Our bodies have their needs, and Islam considers these needs almost sacred because our bodies house our Higher Selves. Thus, the Prophet gently chided his companion Uthman for his austere practices of fasting all day and keeping prayer vigil at night. "Verily, your eyes have rights over you, and your body has its rights, and your family has their rights." Similarly, it is only fair that we take care of our souls. Be mindful and nourish your soul with the life-giving ingredients of love, compassion, silence, beauty, and gratitude.

Equity also demands that we be just with all of God's creation. The Qur'an reminds us several times that as God's representatives on Earth, it is our sacred duty to respect and safeguard the sanctity and rights of animals. They and we have an equal claim to share the Earth's resources (25:48–49, 32:27, 79:31–33) and "they [all] shall be gathered to their Lord in the end" (6:38). How beautiful it is, remarks the Qur'an, that animals and birds "with wings outspread" praise and celebrate God and "each one knows its own [mode of] prayer" (24:41). There are "signs" in the animal world for "those who are wise" (16:68): Consider how God has inspired the bee, says the Holy Book, referring not only to bees' exquisite hives, but also to the way they know how to produce honey from a variety of flowers to delight our sense of taste.

Animals that have not received their fair due in Islam are domestic dogs, falsely believed to be "unclean" and often driven away with stones. The source of this injustice is spurious *ahadith* that are inconsistent with Qur'anic teachings and contradict the Prophet's own example of kindness to dogs, including evidence that he prayed while they cavorted nearby. The contemporary Islamic scholar Abou El Fadl has concluded after exhaustive research that the *ahadith* were passed through questionable chains of transmission and the sayings were actually of pre-Islamic origin. Sadly, traditions that become calcified by time are very slow to change, no matter how unjust or illogical they may be. It cannot be said too often: Justice is closest to God-consciousness, and consciousness of God in all creatures leads to justice.

The call for humans to deal equitably with nature extends to planet Earth and beyond. As early as the seventh century, the Qur'an lamented, "Corruption has appeared on the land and in the sea as an outcome of what human hands have wrought" (30:41). How contemporary that verse seems today, and how sadly we have failed in our responsibility as God's stewards to "walk gently on Earth" (25:63). It is critical that we create a structural shift in our conditioned thinking that allows us to dominate and abuse nature. In a remarkable verse, the Qur'an says, "Greater indeed than the creation of man is the creation of the Heavens and the Earth: yet most men do not understand" (40:57). In a hadith collection by Al-Tabari, the Prophet tenderly implored his community, "The Earth is your mother, so take care of your mother."

Mercy

Justice takes on a divine quality when it is held in the womb of the mother of all divine attributes, compassion. Justice may be the law for humankind, but God "has willed upon Himself the law of grace and mercy" (6:12). "My mercy takes precedence over my wrath," God says in a hadith qudsi. Our work is to evolve into this deeper understanding and practice. To encourage us in that direction, the Prophet conveys God's promise: "Be merciful to those on Earth and He who is in Heaven will be merciful to you."

A news item from Indonesia illustrates this tempering of justice with mercy and responsibility. A judge by the name of Marzuki heard the case of a poor peasant grandmother who stole tapioca from a plantation. The grandmother pleaded guilty and expressed remorse, but explained that her grandchild was severely malnourished and her son, the child's father, was very sick and could not work to feed his child. The plantation manager insisted, however, that she be punished as a deterrent for others. The judge, after expressing regrets to the grandmother, said he had no choice but to follow the law. The grandmother was fined $100 and if she was unable to come up with the sum, she would be jailed for two and a half years. The grandmother wept because it was impossible for her to pay that amount. The judge then removed his hat, put $100 into it, and proceeded to speak: "In the name of justice, I am fining all of you present in court today $5.50 each because, as dwellers of this city, you have allowed a child to starve and forced a grandmother to steal. The registrar will now collect the fines." The news item reported that a total of $200 was collected, and after the fine was paid, the surplus was granted to the grandmother.[2]

REFLECTIONS

Do not barter away your bond with God for a trifling gain.

QUR'AN 16:95

Suppose you rub your ethical skin till it shines, but if inside there is no music—then what?[3]

KABIR

Can you think of times in your life when, despite personal inconvenience and opposition from others, you chose to be just and equitable? How did it feel? If you suffered difficult consequences, how did that affect you?

PRACTICE

The Prophet said, "Everyone sets out each day and trades his soul, either emancipating it or oppressing it." When I am just with someone, my soul is emancipated; when I am unjust, it is oppressed.

Ask yourself the following questions: Am I just with my family members? How do I treat those who can offer me no material or personal advantage? Do I pay attention to and help those who are marginalized, poor, or helpless? Reflect honestly on these questions, and be grateful that you have the gifts of awareness and free will to act justly and compassionately.

GEM 22

"Confound Not Truth with Falsehood"

(QUR'AN 2:42)

WE ALL KNOW IT'S WRONG TO TELL AN OUTRIGHT LIE, except perhaps to save a life, but how many of us indulge in seemingly harmless "little lies" or "truths of convenience"? We don't want to be bothered, so we have the secretary say we're away from the office, or we don't want to face a difficult situation at home so we plead that we have to work overtime. It's in the nature of our untamed ego to twist the truth to our advantage, and many of us do it knowingly and unknowingly, in subtle and overt ways, through exaggeration, lying, denial, or avoidance. Islamic tradition is replete with Mulla stories illustrating our artful ability to stretch and dodge the truth.

One day the Mulla knocked on his neighbor's door and asked to borrow a large pot to prepare food for a large celebration. The neighbor was reluctant to let go of her prized pot, but the unspoken laws of hospitality obliged her to do so. The next day the Mulla returned with two pots: the large one and a smaller one. "Where did the smaller one come from?" asked the housewife. "Madam," said the Mulla, "your pot gave birth to this little one. Didn't you know your pot was pregnant?" "Oh, well," she replied quickly, "I suspected as much," and she thanked him profusely. A few months later the Mulla wanted to borrow the large pot again, and this time the housewife readily acceded. But in the next few days the Mulla didn't return the pot, so she went to his house to collect it. "I'm so sorry, Madam," the Mulla explained, "but your pot was pregnant again and this time she died in childbirth." "That's ridiculous!" retorted the housewife. "How can a pot possibly be pregnant?" "Ah, but you believed it the first time!" he said.

In another story, a neighbor knocked on the Mulla's door, asking to borrow his donkey. The Mulla was unwilling to lend it, so he said, "Brother, I'd like to help you out, but someone else has already borrowed the animal. I wish you had asked earlier." Just at that moment, the donkey in the stable began to bray. "But I hear the donkey!" exclaimed the neighbor. The Mulla, feigning indignation, raised his voice. "Now, who are you going to believe, me or the donkey? And I'm glad we've had this conversation, for I could never lend my donkey to someone who doesn't trust me."

Some of our lies can be quite exotic. The Mulla sneaked over a wall into a rich neighbor's garden and began to fill his sack with a variety of vegetables. The owner chanced to see him and ran over shouting, "What are you doing here?" "Oh," said the Mulla, "I was blown over by a high wind." Looking at the pilfered produce in the Mulla's hands, the owner asked, "And how come the vegetables are uprooted?" "Well, Allah be praised," the Mulla replied. "I was able to grab hold of them to prevent myself from being swept away." "Then why are they in your sack?" demanded the owner. "Indeed," said the Mulla, "life is a mystery. That's exactly what I was wondering before you so rudely interrupted me."

Our lies can also be falsely pious. The Mulla was feasting on a huge roasted chicken when a beggar implored him to share a few bites. "Gladly and willingly," came the reply, "for I believe in sharing, but this chicken unfortunately belongs to my wife. My hands are tied, O hungry friend. I am eating only because my wife has asked me to."

Some of our lies can be absolutely barefaced. A neighbor asked to borrow the Mulla's clothesline, but the Mulla said, "Sorry, it's in use

right now. We're drying wheat flour by putting it on the clothesline."
"Drying flour on the clothesline!" marveled the neighbor. "That
must be a difficult task." "Far less difficult than you'd think if you
don't want to lend the clothesline," replied the shameless Mulla.

These stories are wonderfully amusing and we may snicker that
we ourselves would never bend the truth so brazenly. But the mere fact
that there are so many of them suggests that we are more prone than
we may like to think to shade the truth to our advantage. Spiritual
teachers insist that our understanding and practice of ethics is flawed
if we allow ourselves to deviate from the truth just because "everyone
does it," and they warn that our seemingly innocent little falsehoods
are not truly harmless, for they harm our very souls. We find that we
have hurt ourselves as well as others, and have even perhaps lost the
trust of our loved ones. A little lie here, a little fib there, and soon we
discover that we have become a little blinded here, a little disabled
there in our ability to walk the path of truthfulness. "Confound not
truth with falsehood, nor knowingly conceal the truth" (2:42), says
the Qur'an. And again, "Shun the word that is false" (22:30).

REFLECTIONS
AND
PRACTICE

Examine your attitude about little lies and truths of convenience. List the small prevarications you concoct in the course
of the day. Look at them gently and start a compassionate
campaign to diminish them. Little by little, align them to your
truth in the many opportunities that come your way.

"All Things Have We Created in Proportion and Measure"

(QUR'AN 54:49)

IN THE UNPREDICTABLE TERRAIN OF OUR LIVES, A GOOD sense of balance keeps us on our feet and safely on the path. To appreciate the primal necessity of balance, we simply need to observe the natural world around us. The measured cycles of the seasons are beautiful and life-giving. The cold of December can be grim and yet kind, says Rumi, while summer is all laughter and yet it burns. Without sun and rain in proportion, crops would fail and we would starve. Earth cannot be made into a brick without water, Rumi says in another metaphor, but neither can it become a brick if there is too much water. A bird that cannot open and close its wings cannot fly. The balance between expansion and contraction of our hearts is what keeps us alive. And so it is with all of life: "All things have We created in proportion and measure," God says in the Qur'an, and without the divine sense of balance, all would be chaos and confusion. "The Sun is not permitted to overtake the Moon, nor can the night go beyond the day, but each moves in its lawful way" (36:40).

These signs in nature reflect the need for measure and proportion in our lives. For example, we desperately need balance between work and rest. Spending a disproportionate amount of time in prayer or public service without joyful repose with family and friends makes a person unbalanced and saps our vitality. Muslims address this need for balance in our personal lives by designating Friday a day of rest, community prayer, and family time.

Life brings us blessings and difficulties, and with them come joys and sorrows. A sense of balance allows us to meet the challenges without wasting energy trying to resist them, and to enjoy the blessings without inordinate exultation. Everything is fleeting, the Qur'an suggests, so "don't despair about things that pass you by nor exult over blessings that come to you" (57:23). Sometimes we complain disproportionately about our difficulties. The sage Rabia met a man who had wrapped a large colored bandage around his head and was moaning aloud about his headache. She inquired about his welfare, and he replied that his health was generally good, but on that day he had been gripped by this pain in his head. Rabia expressed sympathy, but then she asked a pointed question: In all his years of sound health, did he wear colors around his head and rejoice aloud in gratitude for his blessings?

Relationships with our fellow human beings often require a fine sense of balance between humility and self-respect, especially when people are rude or abusive. The Qur'an reminds us that "the servants of [Allah] Most Gracious are those who walk on Earth with humility and when the ignorant address them, they say, 'Peace!'" (25:63). Don't oppress others, Sufi teachers say, but don't allow yourself to be abused. Our noble aspirations to walk the path of peace are most effective when they are balanced with practical wisdom, as illustrated in the Sufi teaching story about a snake that was terrorizing a village. A sage known for his ability to communicate with animals spoke persuasively to the snake, and the remorseful creature made a commitment to practice nonviolence. Many months later the sage passed through the village and found the snake in a ragged and pitiable condition. "O seer, what did you teach me?" complained the snake bitterly. "Children practice throwing stones at me, and grown-ups delight in kicking me." "O snake," replied the holy man, "I simply asked you to stop biting. When did I ever ask you to stop hissing?"

Graciousness and generosity are the hallmarks of a spiritually evolved human being, but once again, it is wise to cultivate balance in these virtues. A hand that is always open is as useless as one that is always closed. The Universe does not want us to overdo. Knowing when to stop is a sacred art. There is a charming story about the seventh-century Islamic caliph Harun al Rashid, who complimented an old farmer for so painstakingly planting date palm saplings, which take decades to bear fruit. The hunched old man commented, "We eat from those our forebears planted, so we must plant for those who come after us." The words impressed the caliph and he tossed the old man a purse of gold coins. "Allah be praised!" the old man exclaimed. "These saplings have borne fruit already." Touched by the sincerity of his words, the caliph gave him another purse of coins. Said the old man, "Allah be praised again! Trees normally bear fruit only once a year, but these have produced two crops in one year!" The caliph offered him yet another purse, then turned to his aide and said quietly, "Quick, let's get out of here before the old man leaves us penniless!"

Moderation

Perhaps the most troublesome example of an ego on overdrive and balance gone awry is the inordinate attachment many of us have to the institution of our religion. "We have created you a moderate nation" (2:143), God says in the Qur'an, and follows that up with the command to "commit no excesses in your religion" (4:171). To Muslims overly zealous in advocating the virtues of Islam, the Holy Book advises, "Call thou [all humankind] unto thy Sustainer's path with wisdom and earthly exhortation, and argue with them in the most kindly manner: for behold, thy Sustainer knows best as to who strays from His path, and best knows He as to who are the right-guided"

(16:125). Spiritual teachers rebuke self-righteous and aggressive proselytizers who insist that Muhammad is the greatest of prophets and that Islam is superior to all other religions. Muslims naturally have deep affection for Muhammad, just as the adherents of other religions revere their founders and prophets, but the Qur'an explicitly warns us not to make any distinction between the innumerable prophets sent to People of the Book—Jews, Christians, and Muslims alike (2:136, 2:285). It is the inflated ego that believes one religion is better than all others, and the Holy Book puts that ego in its place. "To each of you We prescribed a law and an open way" (5:48), God says in the Qur'an, implying that beliefs and practices may vary from one community to another. Indeed, the verse continues, we humans could have been created as one single community with a single religion, but instead God chose to create diverse communities with diverse spiritual paths. All that truly matters is that "the goal of you all is [strive to reach] to God; it is He that will show you the truth of the matters in which ye dispute" (5:48).

In a similar vein, spiritual teachers warn us not to overreact when someone criticizes our religion. Again, it is our ego that is bruised, not our religion. If someone spits at the majesty of the sky, Rumi asks, does it stain the sky? "This religion is strong," said the Prophet Muhammad, "so go through it with gentleness."

At an interfaith conference some years ago, a number of Muslim, Jewish, and Christian participants began sharing stories from their traditions about Abraham, Ismail, Isaac, Sarah, Hagar, and Moses. At a certain point, the balanced discussion turned into a heated argument and voices rose as egos became inflamed. The observers became uncomfortably quiet, except for a Native American professor from New York University, who began laughing so hard that someone finally asked him what was so funny. "You know," he said, "we Native Americans also have stories. The only difference is that you guys believe the stories!"

REFLECTIONS

Describe an incident where you overreacted to a comment about religion. How did you overreact and why?

Are there areas of your faith tradition that you feel particularly sensitive about when challenged? If so, what are they?

PRACTICE

Carve out a dedicated time each week to renew your spirit by communing with your Creator, yourself, and your loved ones. Check on your sense of balance during a quiet moment in your day of rest, and resolve to make any necessary adjustments in the days ahead. "Do not deprive yourself of the good things that God has made lawful for you, but commit no excess" (5:87).

GEM 24

"Work in the Invisible World at Least as Hard as You Do in the Visible"

(RUMI)

MUHAMMAD'S *LAILAT AL MIRAJ*, THE NIGHT JOURNEY, has enchanted Muslims and inspired many questions over the centuries. Did the Prophet literally fly from Mecca to Jerusalem and ascend the seven levels of Heaven, as legend would have it, or did he have a mystical vision, similar to the visions, dreams, and allegories reported in all the world's great scriptures? No one knows for sure, and "facts" are not the issue here. What is important is that this mysterious journey has given rise to profound spiritual insights.

Perhaps the greatest insight is the possibility—indeed, the necessity—of working in the invisible world. The Qur'an is full of allusions to the invisible realms. Sufi masters rhapsodize about the world beyond the veil and Rumi urges us to direct as much energy there as we do in our daily lives: Work in the invisible world at least as hard as you do in the visible. According to Sufi teachers, the horizontal journey from Mecca to Jerusalem represents our level of earthly reality as we participate in the daily bazaar of life, while the vertical journey symbolizes our connection to the invisible world through practices that nourish and nurture our souls, such as meditation, prayer, music, and attention to our dreams. Some may be skeptical of talk about the invisible world, but the truth is that the very things that make us truly human are invisible. It is not our bodies that long for beauty, truth, justice, and love. No, it is our souls, which are hidden from sight but make their reality known by their undeniable longings—and the things they long for are themselves invisible, except as they are manifested in transitory form. One evening the ninth-century Sufi master Bayazid Bistami was about to begin his teaching about the mysteries of the invisible world to an assembled crowd. Sitting in front of him was a child with a lighted candle. He asked the child, "Where does the light come from?" The child looked at Bistami and the flame, quickly blew out the candle, and answered, "You tell me, where did it go?"

Spiritual teachers in many traditions agree that both visible and invisible realms are sacred and essential. Look closely at the lotus flower, a symbol of spirituality in the East, and you will see that it has a stem that connects it to the Earth. It is the mud of daily existence that gives life to the beautiful flower. The Qur'an tells us, "Seek the home of the hereafter," but also cautions, "forget not thy portion in this world" (28:77). If we work only in the visible world, we are no more than what Sufi teachers call "wretched employees," but if we toil only in the invisible realms, the same teachers ask, "Why are you here on Earth?" Indeed, Islamic practice does not encourage asceticism and withdrawal from the physical world. It simply reminds us not to devote ourselves excessively or exclusively to the things of this world. In Rumi's pointed metaphor, the visible world is "a place of expenditure," whereas the invisible world is "a place of income." If we are truly invested in becoming our truest, most God-like selves, we will exert equal effort in both realms of endeavor.

One way to do this is to bring the resources of the invisible world to bear on issues we might be experiencing in the visible world. Say you're having a conflict with someone at work or at home and you want to resolve it by talking things over calmly, with honesty and compassion for both yourself and the other party. To prepare yourself for the conversation, it is wise to use prayer, meditation, and silence to create peace and harmony within. Sufi teachers also recommend a psychospiritual exercise called Expression and Resolution, in which you can converse openly with the soul of that person in the invisible realm (some like to call it the "imaginative" realm). In those realms you have permission to express your feelings and thoughts to this person fully and freely. Souls love the truth and your authentic expressions create healing and empowerment for everyone. From my years of psychospiritual counseling, I can say that the work we do in those mysterious realms impacts events in the visible world. Those who do this exercise in the invisible realm before they engage the person often report that they experience a positive shift in themselves. Sometimes they no longer need to confront the person in real time, and if they do go ahead with a live conversation, it goes much better than they had anticipated. This practice is also extremely useful if you have unfinished business with someone who is no longer alive or who is unavailable for person-to-person resolution. If you feel comfortable, you may wish to try the ancient Sufi practice of Expression and Resolution detailed below.

REFLECTIONS
AND
PRACTICE

SETTING THE STAGE FOR THE PRACTICE OF EXPRESSION AND RESOLUTION

In a state of meditation or stillness, usher yourself into your sacred sanctuary (see "Practice" in Gem 20). Savor the safety and beauty of this place, then summon your inner Circle of Love. Remember that each member loves and supports you unconditionally. Give yourself permission to be loved, nurtured, and nourished by your Circle. It is in their nature to love you. Maybe they touch, hold, and embrace you. Spend some time basking in their love and caring for you.

When you are ready, have your Circle of Love summon the soul of the person with whom you are having a difficult issue that you would like to resolve. The person's soul arrives and asks you to experience whatever feelings his or her presence evokes.

EXPRESSION

Give yourself permission to experience your feelings with mercy for yourself. Locate the physical sensations of feelings in your body. With compassion for yourself, little by little, embrace your feelings with your consciousness.

When you sense that the time is right, use these feelings as a bridge to connect to other times you have experienced these feelings with someone else. Always take your Circle of Love with you, and with compassion for yourself, heighten your awareness of those situations in the past. After some time, return to your sanctuary and, with the eyes of the heart, become compassionately aware of how this issue has affected you.

Start the process of speaking to the person with whom you have the issue. Remember that souls love the truth. His or her soul asks you to express your feelings and thoughts with emotion and as fully as possible. Take your time but do not overdo it.

In the next step, express your sacred prayer in the presence of the Universe and the person's soul. What is it you want or need in relation to this person? State your heartfelt desire in the form of a prayer. End the prayer with the sentence, "This,

or whatever is in my highest interest, is manifesting for me
now."

RESOLUTION

Continuing your meditation, tell this person, from your heart,
that he or she is, or has been, in your life as part of a larger,
mysterious story, beyond human faculties to fully understand.

Create a ritual of cutting cords between that person and
yourself. Cut or remove the cords that are unhealthy and
therefore unnecessary. Know that whatever cords need to remain intact will remain so, because the subconscious and the
Circle of Love take care of that part. Participate in the ritual
of cutting cords freely and unabashedly.

As an option, you also have the power to create fresh
cords with this person, heart to heart and soul to soul. These
cords are whole and rooted in Spirit. Please do this only if it
feels right to you.

Listen for the soul of the other person expressing
deep gratitude to you for doing this work of healing and
empowerment.

That person's soul requests permission to be released.
Give your permission, and see and sense the person fading
from your vision and going into the embrace of Spirit as his
or her soul continues to express gratitude to you.

Give yourself permission to be embraced and loved by
your Circle of Love. Then, after a period of nurturance and
nourishment, come back into awareness.

"Move from Knowledge of the Tongue to Knowledge of the Heart"

(TRADITIONAL SAYING)

SECOND ONLY TO *ALLAH* IN THE NUMBER OF TIMES IT IS mentioned in the Qur'an is the world *ilm* ("knowledge"). Thus the search for knowledge is a sacred quest and the Qur'an bids us to pray, "O my Sustainer! Advance me in knowledge" (20:114). "If anyone travels a path of knowledge," said the Prophet, "God will conduct him through one of the paths of paradise; angels will lower their wings ... and the fish in the depths of the water will seek forgiveness for him." So inspiring are these Qur'anic and Prophetic admonitions that for a thousand years Muslims were moved to excel in every field of endeavor, from art, architecture, and literature to the sciences both natural and mystical. Sadly, the quest for knowledge in Muslim countries has been stagnant for the past three hundred years, owing to political turmoil and socioeconomic decline, but there are hopeful signs that a new wave of scholars, including many women, may revitalize and enhance the Muslim contribution to the world's store of knowledge and wisdom.

It is commonly said that the interpretation of information is knowledge, and that the experiential and heartfelt understanding of knowledge leads to wisdom. Of knowledge, the world already has a vast supply; of wisdom, maybe not so much. We have only to look at the sorry state of Mother Earth to see that technological knowledge without the wisdom to use it responsibly is a dangerous thing. Or consider the countless volumes of theological teachings from every religion under the Sun in light of the fact that so few adherents can follow the simple command to love one another. In all facets of life, and particularly in our spiritual lives, we desperately need to move from what Sufi masters call "knowledge of the tongue" (facts, data, and know-how found in books) to "knowledge of the heart," the wisdom to see and honor God in all we say and do.

While the accumulation of knowledge about faith and spirituality is essential for our understanding, it is important to simultaneously persevere with practices that expand our mind and heart. Otherwise, our ego grows impressed with the heights of our accumulated knowledge, and we are in danger of lapsing into what teachers call "scholarly vertigo." As Rumi warns, we engage in unnecessary hairsplitting discussions and arguments. We become like a bird that learns to tie and untie a knot around its legs. Repeatedly, the bird creates more and more complex snares around its legs and cleverly unfastens them to show off its strange skill, forgetting that the point of its knowledge is to escape! We forget that the point of all our spiritual learning is to enjoy what Rumi calls "the joy of sailing the mountain air and savoring the sweetness of the high meadows."

Heart Knowledge

It is one thing to be impressed with our accumulated knowledge for its own sake, but quite another to experience the sacred power of knowledge at the heart level. There is a popular story about a simple village imam who was berated by a theologian for being unlettered in Arabic, the language of the Qur'an. The imam, out of a sincere love of the Holy Book, entreated the theologian to tutor him, and the theologian reluctantly agreed. On the first day of the private lessons, the teacher wrote the letter *Alif,* the first letter of the alphabet, on the blackboard. The pious imam was so deeply moved by the sheer beauty of that single stroke that he burst into tears and asked the surprised professor to end the lesson so he could spend time with the letter. When he appeared for his second lesson, the scholar asked sarcastically if he had mastered the first letter. Face radiant and eyes aglow, the imam lovingly held the chalk and went to the board. As he made the stroke, the board crumbled into pieces! Such is the power of knowledge when infused with love from the heart.

The person with heart knowledge values experience and does not place a premium on mere theory. One way to enrich theory with experience is to pay attention and truly listen. Rumi says that an intellectual aspires to collect data and link them together, but the heart-centered aspirant puts his or her head on a person's chest and "sinks into the answer." Another way to gain heart knowledge is to travel the vast expanse of God's Earth and experience its wondrous diversity of landscapes, peoples, cultures, religions, and beliefs. The Qur'an reminds us that countless peoples have traveled "through the land" so that their hearts and minds "may thus learn wisdom and their ears may thus learn to hear" (22:46). Even the busy bee "finds with skill the spacious paths of its Lord" (16:69) to fulfill its special purpose on this Earth. "Verily in this is a Sign for those who give thought [those who think deeply]" (16:69).

It is in "giving thought" that we begin to understand the incredible power and beauty of knowledge of the heart. "Everywhere you turn is the Face of Allah" (2:115), says the Qur'an, and it is the loving heart that knows how true this is. We may not literally see the face of God, but the Prophet said we can "know Him by His signs." Look at the signs in nature. The Sun and Moon steadily proceeding in their appointed ways (36:40) demonstrate God's constancy. "Look at what happens with a love like that," Hafiz exults: "It lights up the whole

sky!" It is easy enough to see signs of God in things that are pleasant
or beautiful, but our teachers remind us that God even appears with
the face of Satan. How could it be otherwise, if God is all that is? The
knowing heart can accept and live with this shocking idea because it
recognizes the need for both the devil and angelic spirits so that we
might awaken our power of choice and bolster our inner qualities of
restraint, discernment, patience, and right action.

In fact, this ability to comprehend the meanings and values of
diametrically opposed pairs seems to be part of the divine plan.
"Of all things We have created opposites, so that you might bear in
mind [that God alone is One]" (51:49), God says in the Qur'an. The
pains and sorrows in our lives make happiness that much lovelier by
contrast. Rumi says that God turns us from one feeling to another,
so that we might have two wings to fly, not one. Teachers ask us to
ponder the subtle truth that mercy is hidden in wrath and wrath is
hidden in the core of mercy. Indeed, the spaciousness of the human
heart embraces the bewildering paradox of duality. The Creator
"imparted to Adam the nature of all things" (2:31), says the Qur'an,
which spiritual teachers interpret to mean that we humans are endowed with the grace of inner knowing. When we do our inner work,
we begin to comprehend the signs all around us.

One of the most precious manifestations of heart knowledge is
the ability to distinguish between form and essence. All form will
perish, says the Qur'an; all that will abide forever is essence, "the
Face of thy Lord—full of Majesty, Bounty, and Honor" (55:26–27).
In a workshop on this topic in our community, an elegant middle-
aged woman talked about her youthful investment in her physical
beauty, to the point that her identity was totally wrapped up in her
appearance. As her physical form changed with age, she experienced
a devastating identity crisis. Only when her heart began to invest
in the infinite beauty of love, compassion, and service did she find
peace and fulfillment. Several men at the workshop spoke about
their obsessive attachment to the pursuit of money. They experienced

roller-coaster dizziness in loss and gain. They began to ask themselves why they yearned for money and realized their wanting was rooted in a need for freedom, security, and love. When they began to focus on their needs of essence rather than the form of money, not only did their financial situations stabilize, but they also found that many unexpected doors of opportunities for fulfillment opened for them.

The discerning heart also knows there is a difference between pleasure and bliss. God wants us to enjoy the good things in life (Qur'an 7:31), but bliss is our birthright! We are asked to expand our heart knowledge for our own abiding enjoyment. In my small hometown in Bangladesh, Muslim spiritual elders invoke the story of the rural nineteenth-century Hindu sage Ramakrishna to illustrate this point. Ramakrishna would sometimes venture into liquor stores in upscale sections of Calcutta and tell the customers that the intoxication they yearned for was beautiful, but they deserved intoxication of a higher kind. "Get drunk on the real Wine!" he used to tell them. "Become ecstatic on Love, Wonder, Beauty, and Awe!" It is reported that he also went to perfume stores and reassured the patrons that their enjoyment of fragrance was lovely, but if they went deeper, they could go wild on real Fragrance! "Earthly flowers fade," Rumi exclaims, "but flowers that bloom from the heart—what a joy!"

And finally, the enlightened heart knows the wisdom of the famous Qur'anic *sura* (chapter) known by the name *'Asr* ("Time"): "By the token of time, verily humankind is in loss, except such as have faith, and do righteous deeds, and join together in the mutual teaching of truth, and of patience and constancy" (103:1–3). All the time we spend in the pursuit of knowledge is virtually wasted if we do not infuse that knowledge with the heart qualities of patience, humility, and loving-kindness. On the other hand, if we have truly moved from knowledge of the tongue to knowledge of the heart, we will share that knowledge humbly with our faith communities in the cause of justice, righteousness, and healing for our troubled world.

REFLECTIONS

Earthly flowers fade but flowers that bloom from the heart—what a joy!

RUMI

External theological learning moves like a moon and fades when the Sun of experience comes up.

SANAI, TWELFTH-CENTURY SUFI POET

Which of your beliefs come from personal reflection, explorations, and experiences, rather than hearsay and tradition? Are these ever in conflict with one another?

What do you do when you experience a conflict between conventional interpretation and your personal understanding of some aspect of a sacred text?

PRACTICE

When you are weighing options for an important decision, remember the Prophet's advice: "Consult your heart! Consult your heart! Consult your heart!"[1] With eyes closed, lovingly focus on your heart and intend to breathe through it. Allow divine Breath to caress you in that space. Then, place each option separately in your heart and become aware of the feelings that arise. "Closest to the light," and therefore the wisest option, is the one that evokes a feeling of inner peace and joy.

"Whoever ... Believes in God Has Grasped the Most Trustworthy Handhold"

(QUR'AN 2:256)

THE ABILITY TO BELIEVE AND TRUST IN SOMEONE greater than our human ego or something greater than a human institution is fundamental to the kind of inner peace we need to sustain us on our path. We may not feel an urgent need for God in happy times, but we shall certainly desire that "trustworthy handhold" when we grapple with failures and afflictions. When we strive to build faith and trust in God, we shall find that God has "endeared" our faith to us and "made it beautiful in [our] hearts" (49:7). This is not about the kind of faith prescribed by catechisms and creeds; this is about the deep inner certainty, the heart knowledge that our lives are part of a larger story that is constantly unfolding by grace of a compassionate Creator. Even staunch nonbelievers practice a kind of faith. There is an amusing story about an atheist who told his son there is no God. Having been taught to question everything he heard, the boy shot back, "But Dad, how do you know?" Replied his father, "You just have to take it on faith, my son!"

Trust in God and God-Given Gifts

Without faith, life may be marked by chronic anxiety. Rumi tells the story of a "sweet-mouthed" cow who chomps and munches on the grass all day until the field is emptied. At night the cow worries excessively, "O my, what will I eat tomorrow?" and becomes "thin as a hair from anxiety." The next morning the field is filled with grass and the cow eats its full meal again, but at night the same story: The cow is feverish with panic about what it will eat tomorrow. Of course, the grass grows again. The Qur'an reminds us that our Sustainer is "the One who sends down rain after they have lost all hope" (42:27) and "has made in service to you all that is in the Heavens and on Earth" (31:20). Christians know about divine generosity from Jesus's beautiful advice on the Mount of the Beatitudes: "Do not worry about your life, what you will eat or what you will drink.... Look at the birds of the air; they neither sow nor reap nor gather into barns, and yet your heavenly Father feeds them. Are you not of more value than they?" (Matthew 6:25–26). Jews, too, know from their sacred scriptures that the Holy One provides for us as well as for the birds of the air: "They that wait for the Lord shall renew their strength, then shall mount up with wings as eagles" (Isaiah 40:31).

We live in a practical and pragmatic culture that sets great store by the folk saying "God helps those who help themselves," and the Prophet said virtually the same thing back in the seventh century. A Bedouin asked Muhammad whether he should first tie his camel to a post and then go into the mosque to pray, or should he trust in God that the camel would be there when he came out of the mosque. Replied the Prophet, "First tie your camel to the post, then trust in God." In spiritual matters, God is indeed a most trustworthy handhold, but in daily matters we are expected to engage our God-given intelligence to recognize and use the gifts God has provided for our needs. Take, for example, the story of a traveler who successfully negotiated a scorching desert, a steep mountain, and a dark forest before arriving at a fast-flowing river. He cast his creative eyes around and found bamboo and vines, from which he constructed a small raft to get across the river. God provided the means, we might say, and the traveler helped himself.

But then, when he reached the other side, the traveler forgot about trusting God to provide for a future need. Hoisting the raft on his shoulders, he continued his journey, weighed down by an unnecessary burden. The practical among us may point out that the traveler was simply being prudent. What if he came to another river where there were no vines and reeds with which to make another raft? How burdensome it is to live in a perpetual state of "what if"! Rumi tells us to pause and ask ourselves if we personally planned out all the mysteries of our conception, arrival on Earth, and the twists and turns of life that have brought us to the present moment. Of course we didn't, and yet by grace of God, here we are. In the same way and "with exactly the same mercy and mystery and strange providence," Rumi says, we shall be brought to "thousands of other worlds." Have faith, therefore, for "God is the protector of those who have faith" (2:257) and "with Him are the keys of the Unseen, the treasures that none know but He" (6:59).

The Role of Hope in Faith

Faith in a compassionate and provident Creator leads naturally to hope, a virtue famously described by the mystic poet Emily Dickinson as:

> *the thing with feathers*
> *That perches in the soul,*
> *And sings the tune without the words,*
> *And never stops at all.*

No matter that we don't know all the words: As long as we can hum the tune of divine love at the heart of our soul, we need never lose hope in the vitality and meaning of our lives. Even when we fly through the Valley of Bewilderment, like Attar's birds on their journey to the Simorgh (Gem 7), our hope and trust in union with the Beloved keep us on the wing. "Never lose hope, my heart!" cried Rumi. Know that miracles dwell in the invisible realms and even if the whole world turns against you, "Keep your eyes on the Friend." The Qur'an says, "If Allah helps you, none can overcome you: If He forsakes you, who is there, after that, who can help you?" (3:160).

How essential is hope? Take it from the Mulla, who saw the ticket conductor walking toward him on a crowded train. Hurriedly, he began to look for his ticket, but in other people's pockets. The puzzled and irritated passengers finally asked why he didn't look in his own pocket. "Indeed, I could do that," the Mulla said, "but if I don't find the ticket there, I shall lose all hope!"

Let us end this reflection on the virtues of faith and hope with a celebrated Sufi teaching story about a stream that passed through several landscapes of the country and came to a desert. It had pushed through barriers before, but now the harder it pushed, the more its waters disappeared. It knew that its destiny was to cross the desert, but how? A voice from the desert whispered, "The wind crosses the desert, and it can carry you to your destination." The voice told the stream to allow itself to be absorbed in the wind, but this was unacceptable to the stream. Being absorbed meant it would have to give up its individuality. And what assurance was there that the wind could carry the stream? And if it did reach its destination, would it be the same stream as it is now? Softly, the voice gave assurances that the wind could take it beyond the desert, and at its destination the stream's essence would remain the same, but its form might be different. In fact, said the voice, "You are called what you are today only because you do not know which part of you is the essential one." As the stream pondered its options, certain memories and feelings began to stir and it vaguely remembered being held in the arms of the wind. Finally, trusting in the wind, the stream raised its vapors and the welcoming arms of the wind tenderly bore it across the desert and let it fall softly as rain onto the roof of a mountain far away. By trusting the hand-hold of God, it was able to remember more clearly its true identity and find joy and freedom in the Wind.[1]

REFLECTIONS

And as for those who have attained to faith in Allah and hold fast to Him, He will cause them to enter into His compassion and His abundant blessing, and guide them to Himself by a straight way.

QUR'AN 4:175

Don't you see that God has made in service to you all that is in the Heavens and on Earth and has made His bounties flow to you in abundant measure, seen and unseen?

QUR'AN 31:20

In your life, what events and circumstances deepened your faith in God? When have you mistrusted your faith? What happened to restore your faith?

PRACTICE

With mindfulness and persistence, become aware of aspects of God's creation. For example, observe sunrise and sunset, gaze at moonlight and stars at night, ponder the cycles of seasons, birth, and death. If you feel inspired, express your wonder in art, music, or poetry. Any practice that evokes a sense of awe and wonder connects us to the invisible world and builds faith.

WALKING
ON
SPACIOUS
PATHS

"Women Are the Twin-Halves of Men"

(HADITH)

IN THE ENVIRONMENT OF SEVENTH-CENTURY ARABIA, where women often were treated as chattel and female infanticide was not uncommon, the Prophet's declaration of equal personhood for women was unacceptable to many tribal men. They stifled their objections while the Prophet was alive, but after his death they reasserted their dominance over women, mainly by concocting spurious hadith. But evidence of the Prophet's high regard for women is there for all to see in many genuine hadith, and overriding all human opinions are the words of the Holy Qur'an, enshrining the status of women alongside men in the nascent Muslim community: "The Believers, men and women, are protectors, one of another" (9:71). For example, in a radical departure from seventh-century patriarchal norms, the Qur'an granted women property, divorce, and inheritance rights, and asserted, "Women shall have rights similar to the rights against them" (2:228) ["the rights against them" refers to marriage and divorce rights]. Seconding the Qur'an are Muhammad's instructions to his community: "Women are the twin-halves of men" and "The rights of women are sacred. See to it that they are maintained in the rights assigned to them."

Sadly, a number of Muslim legal scholars over the centuries, for a variety of historical reasons, have blatantly misinterpreted Qur'anic verses so that they oppress the very women they were meant to protect. As a result, the status of women in Islamic cultures today is decidedly second-class. I have written extensively on this topic in other books (*Out of Darkness into Light* with Kathleen Elias and Ann Holmes Redding; *Religion Gone Astray* [SkyLight Paths] with Pastor Don Mackenzie and Rabbi Ted Falcon), so I will not repeat the list of injustices here. Instead, I would like to focus on the need for healing of the deep wound in the cultural traditions of Islam. The subject is complex because the situation varies in different cultures and countries, but overall the Muslim psyche is deeply paralyzed because of the disempowerment of women.

Spiritual teachers have called for sacred dialogue in which men and women listen to one another's pain and sufferings. However, since the bias in Islamic culture is overwhelmingly against women, it is we men who must truly listen to the women in our own families, in schools and places of work, and in the community. It is essential that Muslim men create an environment in which the women in our lives feel safe to express their feelings on the issue of inequality without fear of judgment and retribution. Further, it behooves us to listen carefully to the growing number of female scholars who are challenging traditional patriarchal interpretations of the Qur'an. Men have held that prerogative exclusively for so long that patriarchal bias has become institutionalized. This is the bias that interprets Arabic words, according to a meaning that is most favorable to men. Consider the controversial verse on "wife beating" that has given so much grief to women. The verse states that if the wife is suspected of disobedience and infidelity, the husband has a right to "beat" her (4:34). The verse hinges on the translation of the root word *daraba*. Arabic words have many nuanced meanings.

Historically, most men have translated the word as "beat," but most women scholars today translate it as "turn away from"; in other words, take time away from each other until the matter has been resolved. In any case, we should have the spiritual strength and grace to say that, in this day and age, there is no "divine right" sanctioned by the Holy Book to treat one's wife in a way that is inhumane, illegal, and unacceptable.

Muslim women in our community point to two other revelations that positively support the equal worth of women. One occurred after the Prophet lamented to God that he had no surviving male heirs, a considerable social hardship in that patriarchal society. Immediately, the Almighty responded: "To thee have We granted the fount [of Abundance]. Therefore to thy Lord turn in prayer and sacrifice" (108:1–2). This is an extraordinary verse, for the message is that fullness of life comes not from meeting tribal and patriarchal expectations, but from being conscious of God and bringing a heart turned in devotion and service to our Creator. The other revelation occurred after Umm Salama, a wife of the Prophet, questioned why the revelations always seemed to be addressed only to men. Again the response from the Heavens was immediate: "For men and women who surrender themselves to God ... and for men and women who remember God unceasingly, for them God has readied forgiveness and a supreme recompense" (33:35).

There is, in fact, a strong vein of gender equality in the Qur'an, starting with the story of the first couple's fall from grace in the Garden of Eden. In the Bible story, the serpent tempts Eve and she then tempts Adam to join her in eating the forbidden fruit, so that women in Judeo-Christian societies have borne the stigma ever since. In the Qur'an, there is no suggestion that "the woman" caused Adam to sin. Both were equally beguiled into making wrong choices. "As a result, they both ate of the tree" (20:121), both suffered the consequences, both apologized profusely (7:23), and both were promised ongoing love and guidance by the Creator.

Even more important than the original fall from grace in Islamic belief is the Day of Judgment, when all will be called to account for the way they spent their precious days on Earth. Here, according to the Qur'an, the terrible wrong done to female infants will be the first item on the agenda. The innocent souls of baby girls that were buried alive will be raised up and asked, "For what crime were you killed?" (81:8–9). This passage can also be seen as a metaphor for the suppression of women's rights, with the underlying message that the crime of suppressing women's basic rights has the highest priority in the divine court of justice.

Steps toward Healing

A major step toward healing the divide between Muslim men and women is for more of us to recognize and celebrate the divine feminine principle that runs deep in Islam. Divine Essence is called *Al-Dhat,* a feminine word in Arabic. The primary divine attributes are *rahman* and *rahim* (compassion and mercy), both derived from the Semitic root *rhm,* meaning "womb." Another important word for God, *Al-Hikmah* (Wisdom), is also feminine. Muslim poets and sages throughout the centuries have referred to God in the feminine gender. The Kabah toward which Muslims bow down in prayer is described as "a bride veiled in mystery." The magical steed that bore Muhammad on the *miraj* invariably has a female face, leading many scholars of Eastern religions to surmise that it was the feminine kundalini energy that propelled the Prophet on his mysterious journey. And all Muslims—male and female alike—are called to "give birth" to our "inner Jesus," which we can do only by nurturing the womb of our inmost heart. This calls on us to cultivate the feminine qualities of compassion, forbearance, and nurturance. Indeed, the womb merits special regard in the Qur'an. In the first verse of a chapter called "The Women," the Holy Book tells us to reverence God and reverence the wombs that bore us (4:1).

Another major step toward healing is to discredit and discard the countless *ahadith* about the Prophet's supposed disdain for women. Not only would he not have said something so hurtful as "But for women, men would have entered Paradise," but what he actually said was, "Paradise lies at the feet of your mother." To appreciate the full meaning of this famous saying, it is helpful to know the context. One of Muhammad's followers came to him and said, "Messenger of God, I want to go on a military expedition and I have come to consult you." What he was really looking for was an opportunity for martyrdom and its heavenly reward. But the Prophet asked the man if his mother was still alive, and upon hearing that she was, he told the man, "Stay with her, for Paradise is at her feet." In other words, the heavenly Paradise can wait. The feminine love that bore us is Heaven on Earth. On another occasion the Prophet said that no matter what we do for our mothers, we never can repay them for even one night's worth of worry. A persistent questioner asked if he would not be re- paying his debt if he carried his infirm mother on his back for years, fed her, and cared for her in every possible way. "There would still be this difference," Muhammad replied: "Your mother served you by yearning for you to live; but you would serve her by waiting for her to die."

The Prophet's devotion to the women in his personal life was legendary. In an age when polygamy was the norm, he was joyously and faithfully married for twenty-five years to his beloved Khadija until she died. A widow when she married Muhammad, Khadija was fifteen years the Prophet's senior and also his social superior. It was she who taught him to be a successful businessman, and it was also she who believed in his Prophetic mission even before he did. Histori- ans recorded the pain he felt at Khadija's death. Working through his tears, he actively participated in every stage of the burial, from digging the grave to laying his beloved wife in it with his own hands. After Khadija's death, Muhammad married several times. Save for Aisha, who was the daughter of his best friend, all the women were socially vulnerable by virtue of divorce, widowhood, or slavery, and he offered them the protection of marriage out of concern for their well-being.

One more major step toward honoring the women of Islam is for couples to recognize the profound spiritual growth and learning that can come from the sacred union of a marriage between equals. "He created for you mates from among yourselves, that ye may dwell in tranquility with them, and He has put love and mercy between your [hearts]" (30:21), says the Qur'an. The Prophet proclaimed that a good marriage is "half of religion," and the poet Rumi offered a blessing on the union of heart and soul:

> *May these vows and this marriage be blessed.*
> *May it be sweet milk,*
> *this marriage like wine and halvah.*
> *May this marriage offer fruit and shade*
> *like the date palm.*
> *May this marriage be full of laughter,*
> *our every day a day in paradise.*
> *May this marriage be a sign of compassion,*
> *a seal of happiness here and hereafter.*
> *May this marriage have a fair face and a good name,*
> *an omen as welcomes the Moon in a clear blue sky.*
> *I am out of words to describe*
> *how Spirit mingles in this marriage.*[1]

May Spirit mingle in the hearts of my sister and brother Muslims so that we may be protectors, supporters, and sincere friends of one another.

REFLECTIONS

The ninth-century sage Rabia was so exquisitely devoted to Allah that women and men adored her, but the clerics envied her. One day the men confronted her and boasted, "The crown of prophethood has been placed on men's heads. The belt of nobility has been fastened around men's waists. No woman has ever been a prophet." "Ah," Rabia replied, "but egoism and self-worship and 'I am your Lord most high' have never sprung from a woman's breast. All these have been the specialty of men."

What are some gender biases you notice in yourself?

What are some gender biases you notice in others, especially family members?

PRACTICE

To heal wounds and create wholeness in our beings, it behooves us to encourage male and female members of our own family to make time to listen, witness, and honor feelings about gender roles and cultural biases that cause personal pain and suffering.

In order to expand my work in the community, I work with and highly recommend Satyana Institute (www.satyanainstitute.org), which offers excellent workshops worldwide on the subject of gender reconciliation.

When talking about God, make a conscious effort to refer to Divinity in the feminine gender as often as in the masculine.

"Come to Know Each Other"

(QUR'AN 49:13)

THE MULLA CALLED HIS FRIENDS TO GATHER ROUND and listen to his exciting new way of playing the violin. With great fanfare he lifted the instrument to his chin and began to play—and play, and play, the same note over and over again! The audience stirred as their discomfort and embarrassment increased, and finally his wife asked him why he didn't move his fingers on the different strings, as other musicians do. "Well," he replied, "those others are all struggling to find the perfect note, but I have already found it!"

Not only is a singular "perfect" note boring and devoid of beauty when it is played repeatedly with no variation, but it can also truly be perfect only when it harmonizes and resonates with other notes. This is why God has showered the Earth with an abundance of diversity. Divinity has designated "for everyone ... a law and way of life" (5:48), created a "diversity of tongues and colors" (30:22), and of the things on this Earth "multiplied in varying hues" (16:13). Our Creator could easily have formed us a single community, says the Qur'an, but instead chose diversity so that we might "strive as in a race in all virtues" (5:48) and enjoy "unity in diversity" (2:148, 21:92–93, 23:52). In our age of both pluralism and polarization, the most commonly quoted Qur'anic verse declares, "O humankind! We created you from a single [pair] of a male and a female and made you into nations and tribes that you might come to know each other" (49:13).

The key Prophetic words are *come to know each other*. To overcome adversity and temper polarization, it is essential to establish a personal and human relationship with the other. The goal is not to change the other's opinion or carry out a secret agenda in creating this bond. Rather, the goal is to listen, respect, and connect, so that it becomes impossible to demonize or dehumanize the other. Even if our differences in politics or ideology remain unaltered as we come to know the other, we no longer perceive the other as a threat.

The proposal to build a mosque and interfaith center at Ground Zero in New York City sparked a national outcry and backlash against a project that would, in the eyes of some, dishonor the memory of those killed on 9/11 by Islamic terrorists or further an insidious plot to "Islamicize" America. A nationwide poll in 2010 showed that 61 percent of people in the United States were opposed to the building project; only 26 percent were in favor of it. The remarkable finding is that each of those opposed said they did not personally know even one Muslim.[1] We also know from previous Gallup polls that "those Americans who know at least one Muslim are more likely to hold positive views of Muslims and Islam."[2] Once again, the need to know the other, especially in times of distrust and doubt, is paramount.

Little Self and Exclusivity

To come to know the other who is different is a Qur'anic injunction, and yet, tragically, few of us, Muslim or non-Muslim, can obey this simple prescription because it is so difficult to grow out of our conditioning and tribalism. We in twenty-first-century America don't like to think of ourselves in terms of that primitive concept—tribalism—and yet that is the underlying cause when we allow ourselves to be trapped by our little selves, which seek comfort in the company of those who look, think, and act the way we do. It is easier and more convenient to ignore or curse the darkness of the unfamiliar than to create the light of friendship, understanding, and cooperation. We cherry-pick and ferret out verses from our scriptures that support our feelings of moral and religious superiority. But the work of connecting with the other was not meant to be easy. The Qur'an points out, as mentioned in a previous chapter, "We have sent some of you to be a trial for others; will you have patience?" (25:20).

We often hear that the things we strongly dislike in others, even in our own tribe, are things we subconsciously dislike about ourselves. Highlighting this powerful insight, the Prophet Muhammad said, "The faithful are mirrors to each other." The obvious cure for being averse to others is to acknowledge, heal, and spiritually integrate their unlikable qualities in ourselves. The work is hard but the benefits are immense. We grow from this difficult but holy endeavor and honor God's plan for creating diversity. The effort makes us more fully human and gives meaning to our lives.

The other reason for our difficulty in genuinely connecting with the other is that we build institutions and traditions around our tribalism and force ourselves to believe overtly and covertly that the institutions and traditions of our culture, politics, and religion are superior. We become condescending in various degrees and believe that our mission is to promote and advocate for our own tribe, and wear down any opposition. Our drumbeats are so loud that we cannot listen to the other. This is especially pervasive in the domain of religion. The important point to glean here is that our institutional bias and exclusivity are simply reflections of our untamed ego. An institution is nothing more than a collection of egos in various stages of development. When we proclaim exclusivity, this is not religion but our ego speaking. Rumi asks us to become still and realize how ugly rings the metallic music of our collective rigidities and certainties. The Qur'an says that God will not change the condition of a people unless they change their inner selves (13:11). There is no escaping or avoiding the inner work.

Sufi teachers make a critical point with regard to institutions. Laypeople surmise mistakenly that the subjects of theology, ideology, and public policy should be left to experts and institutions because the issues are far too subtle or complex for the average person. The truth is that the greatest learning can come from laypeople getting to know the other and sharing teachings and experiences with one another.

A Mulla story speaks to this topic. One day the Mulla was invited to preach at a famous mosque. As he stepped onto the podium, he asked, "Do you know what I'm going to talk about today?"

In one voice the congregation replied, "No," so the Mulla stepped down, saying it would be a waste of his time if they didn't know what he was talking about. Urged by the mosque officials to return, he again ascended the podium and asked the same question. Thinking they had learned their lesson, the congregation replied, "Yes! Yes!" whereupon the Mulla stepped down again, saying that, in that case, there was no need for him to teach. Exasperated, the mosque officials once again pressed him to return and the Mulla once again asked the same question. "Do you know what I'm going to talk about today?" Chastened by their previous experience, some in the congregation said "Yes" and others said "No."

"Very well," said the Mulla, as he stepped down from the podium again. "Those who said 'yes' teach the ones who said 'no.'"

How can we talk to those who fervently believe their religion is the only way to God? This question comes up repeatedly during interfaith programs and presentations. The answer is to acknowledge and honor others' beliefs as long as they are not violently imposed on us. Our spiritual work is not to change others' views but to bond on a human level. Similarly, we are not asked to cave in to others' proselytizing, but simply to get to know differently believing people on a human level and collaborate on two pressing issues that are close to all our hearts: social justice and care of Mother Earth. Debating about ideology will take us to dead ends, but developing friendships will enable us to join hands for the common good, regardless of our religious and theological differences. Almost invariably, personal relationships are the gateway to collaboration. Take, for example, the Habitat for Humanity program, in which people of all faiths and political persuasions—diehard conservatives and liberals alike—collaborate in building homes for the poor. Beliefs and ideologies may be poles apart, but everyone who participates in such a program is motivated by a universal imperative to extend justice, loving-kindness, and opportunities to those marginalized by life circumstances.

In the process of working together and getting to know each other, minds and hearts open up. In my life, for example, through my abiding friendship with some Christian clerics and laypeople over the years I have become aware of my own biases and narrow stereotyping of Evangelical Christians. I had no idea of the diversity in opinion among them, their willingness to listen, their love of community, and their unwavering dedication to social causes. Friendship with people in these diverse communities has broadened my perspective in ways I could never imagine.

Friendship

In 2011, Brenda Bentz, a dedicated lay leader at St. Mark's Episcopal Cathedral in Seattle, single-handedly brought together a group of religious and lay leaders to initiate and convene a national program on Islamophobia at St. Mark's. When asked why she strained herself so greatly in spite of a chronic illness, she always replied, "Because it matters." I was privileged to be one of three keynote speakers, along with Imam Feisal Raul, leader of the Ground Zero Mosque, and Professor Yvonne Haddad, professor of Islamic history and Christian-Muslim relations at the Alwaleed Bin Talal Center for Muslim-Christian Understanding at Georgetown University. In an e-mail a few days after my talk, Brenda said that my talk was quite good but "more effective" was the workshop I did with Rabbi Ted Falcon that same afternoon. In the workshop, Ted and I

bantered with each other, shared stories and insights, and did inter-
active exercises. But apparently what mattered most was our friendship of eleven years, dating to our interfaith service for peace and
healing in those emotion-filled days following 9/11. In that e-mail,
Brenda reported about a friend of hers who was outraged at the
Israeli treatment of Palestinians. Her friend's heart had hardened
against all Jews, and she couldn't get past her anger. But when the
friend saw Rabbi Ted's love for me, a Muslim, "Something melted
the stone in her heart." Nothing Brenda had said to her friend had
ever touched that stone, "but the palpable love of a rabbi for an
imam did." She ended the e-mail with the following words, "So we
know how effective your work is! And I suspect that it will never be
the volumes you three write as much as it is this work directly with
people." The third person Brenda was referring to is our colleague,
Pastor Don Mackenzie, who was out of town that day. Brenda
Bentz died in May 2012, but her passion for interfaith peace and
love has borne fruit in every Christian, Muslim, and Jew who attended her program and dared to reach out to the "other" in hope,
trust, and mutual regard.

REFLECTIONS

You have created this *I* and *us* to play the game of adoration with Yourself.

RUMI

If I make my religion an obstacle between me and you, I
also make it an obstacle between me and God.

TRADITIONAL SAYING

Do you have personal and social relationships with people
who differ from you in religion, color, culture, political

affiliation, and/or economic status? If so, when feelings of discomfort arise in you, what do you do about these feelings?

PRACTICE

Consider participating in a program such as "Amazing Faiths Dinner Dialogue Project," in which eight to ten invitees from various religions share religious and spiritual experiences. Details can be found at www.amazingfaithsproject.org and at www.interfaithamigos.com.

Create an "Interfaith Cooperative Circle" in your neighborhood, inviting laypeople from different religions to cooperate in projects of social justice and Earth care. For resources and suggestions, consult United Religions Initiative (www.uri.org).

Keep a journal in which you record your feelings and insights as you develop relationships with those who are different from you.

"Be Quick in the Race for Forgiveness from Your Lord"

(QUR'AN 3:133)

THE PROPHET MUHAMMAD WAS KNOWN TO BEG DIVINE forgiveness so frequently day and night that his community called him the "Prince of Forgiveness." His mantra, *Estaghfirullah* (I beg repentance, Allah), is a Sufi favorite that, as mentioned earlier, is a powerful reminder when we have strayed into forgetfulness and have become oblivious to our intention to live as consciously as possible. The word is invoked not out of guilt or fear of punishment but out of contrition for our lack of awareness. Too often we become unmindful and inattentive, causing unintended pain to others and becoming separated from God. It is not only our fellow humans that we wound in our unconsciousness. Sufis point out, for instance, that we have no idea how much pain we cause to the insect and ant community in the simple act of walking through a meadow. A remarkable passage in the Qur'an describes an ant warning the members of its colony, "O ye ants, get into your habitations, lest Solomon and his hosts crush you [under foot] without knowing it" (27:18). This is a wonderfully amusing image (the Qur'an says that Solomon smiled when he heard the ant), but it is also deeply touching. Just a simple act of walking across a lawn—let alone watering, mowing, or weeding it—causes immense panic and suffering among the tiny creatures underfoot. We can choose to dismiss that idea as a charming anthropomorphism, but a better path is to chant *Estaghfirullah* for any unintended harm while treading as consciously as possible wherever we need to go.

All-Merciful God

The Qur'an advises us to "be quick in the race for forgiveness from your Lord" (3:133). Sufis believe that frequent repetition of *Estaghfirullah* from the heart will endear us to the Beloved and bring us closer to Divinity. The Qur'an makes it clear that God loves to forgive whether we offend occasionally, habitually, or exceedingly: "O my servants who have transgressed against their souls! Despair not of the Mercy of Allah: for Allah forgives all mistakes: for He is Oft-Forgiving, Most Merciful" (39:53). This does not mean that we may speak and act without regard for the spiritual consequences of our acts and intentions. The Sufi teacher Al Junayd draws our attention to three conditions for repentance to be accepted.[1] The first is true remorse. The second is a firm resolution not to return to the wrongdoing just as, in the words of the Prophet, "Milk returns not to the udder." The third is the righting of a grievance: "And whoever repents and does good has truly turned to God by repentance" (25:71).

Two grave offenses, according to the Qur'an, are the worship of "gods other than God" and renunciation of Islam after having accepted it. Theologians quibble at length about whether God will ever forgive these sins, especially if the sinners do not repent before they meet their Creator. Sufis generally refuse to be drawn into these dry, hairsplitting discussions. Proponents of every nuanced position will find in the spaciousness of the Qur'an an appropriate verse to support their claim. The wise have said that we do not see things as they are; we see things as we are. God says in the Qur'an, "Of knowledge We have given you but a little" (17:85), and a hadith teaches that God's mercy precedes His wrath. It is not for mere humans to decide who merits divine forgiveness.

Forgiving Others

According to a hadith verified by Abu Hurayrah, Muhammad said that the prophet Moses asked, "O my Lord! Who is the best of Your servants in Your estimation?" God replied, "He who pardons when he is in a position of power." The Prophet, who certainly had the power in his community, readily forgave a woman who had tried to poison him and also acceded to a plea of forgiveness from Wahshi, an enemy who had murdered the Prophet's beloved uncle. In Wahshi's case, Muhammad even allowed him to rejoin the community, but with the warning that he should keep his distance from the Prophet.[2] There is an important teaching here: Forgiveness of the other is noble, essential, and spiritually uplifting, but true forgiveness is not possible unless one has healed and integrated the pain, anger, and suffering caused by the injury, whether it was intended or not. When we honor, heal, and integrate our injured feelings, we are performing acts of compassion and beauty.

Every holy book has verses that challenge us to aspire to seemingly impossible heights. The Qur'an, for example, commands Muslims to repel evil with something better so that an enemy becomes an intimate friend (41:34). Clearly, our Creator has faith that we can grow in consciousness to attain those exalted states. We are asked to expand our awareness and compassion, fully embrace and integrate our anger and pain so that our hearts have the spaciousness to forgive, and reach out with love to our enemy. This might seem unrealistic, but because the injunction is from Divinity, it must be possible to evolve into those celestial states on Earth. Incredible though it may seem, we humans have a divine potential to forgive our enemies.

Seeking Forgiveness and Atonement

It is customary for Muslims to seek forgiveness from others before embarking on Hajj and during the month of purification and renewal known as Ramadan. Like most other people, Muslims also feel the need to ask forgiveness from others as they prepare for their transition to the great beyond.

In my work I see many clients who are burdened by remorse or lack of closure and are longing for forgiveness from someone who has died. Using a form of the Sufi practice Expression and Resolution described in Gem 24, I help them engage with the deceased person in the invisible world. Allah alone is the Knower of the Unseen, but sages and prophets have discerned that, to use Rumi's words, there is traffic and trade in those mysterious realms. In a state of meditation and supported by an inner Circle of Love, the aggrieved person expresses remorse and sorrow to the soul of the departed, asks for forgiveness, and commits to an act of charity "to give freely of what you love" (3:92) in the name of that person. I also encourage my clients to commune with the departed soul and with God in the early hours of the morning, because the Qur'an suggests that that is a propitious time to pray for forgiveness from one's innermost heart (3:17). Almost invariably, the process results in feelings of consolation, tranquility, and closure of unresolved issues. Some even report that they feel the departed soul is now their ally as they continue their walk on Earth.

There are examples of pious beings who humbly and quietly atone for a harm caused to someone by a member of their community. Such is the story of a Pakistani deputy attorney general named Khurshid Khan. In 2010, a member of the minority Sikh community was brutally killed by the Taliban in Pakistan. Mr. Khan, a devout Muslim, feels such deep remorse for the killing by his coreligionists that in any spare time he can muster he visits Sikh temples in Pakistan and India and volunteers to polish the shoes of temple attendants (shoes are considered dirty in the South Asian culture), clean latrines, cook food, and learn scripture from Sikh gurus. Mr. Khan has discerned that what he values most is his time and energy, and he humbly devotes them in service of penance, with full support of his family. Preferring to perform his service anonymously, Mr. Khan agreed to tell his story only when elders assured him that his example would inspire others and that disclosure was for the common good.³

Forgiving Self

Sufi teachers emphasize that our capacity for forgiveness rests ultimately on the ability to forgive ourselves. The words of Carl Jung summarize this critical need most beautifully: "That I feed the hungry, forgive an insult, and love my enemy—these are great virtues. But what if I should discover that the poorest of the beggars and most impudent of offenders are all within me, and that I stand in need of the alms of my own kindness; that I myself am the enemy who must be loved—what then?"⁴

REFLECTIONS

If one is patient in adversity and forgives—this, behold, is something to set one's heart upon.

QUR'AN 42:43

When you intend to forgive someone who has wronged you, or seek forgiveness from someone whom you have wronged, what difficult feelings surface? Can you remember to embrace these difficult feelings with mercy for yourself?

PRACTICE

To forgive yourself using a time-honored practice, focus on the space of your heart, embrace your heart, and talk to it honestly and compassionately about your sadness, guilt, and frustration about yourself. Allow yourself to experience and express whatever feelings surface as you commune with your heart. When you finish, become aware of Divinity inside your heart. Sense your human heart being embraced and consoled by your divine Heart. Using words that resonate for you, tell your heart, "I love you and I forgive you." Divine Heart is speaking through you to your human heart. If you do this often, you will experience a wave of self-assurance and affection enveloping your heart space, and you will also discover that your capacity to love and forgive others has increased exponentially.

Sincerely repeat the word *Estaghfirullah* to Divinity in your heart as a mantra in meditation and during wakeful hours. Practitioners say this expands awareness, bestows inner calm, and nourishes our feelings of closeness to God.

The Qur'an advises us to "celebrate the praises of thy Lord, and pray for His forgiveness" whenever we experience "victory" and "the help of God" (110:1 and 3). Why ask for forgiveness at these times? Because it counters the dangers of our ego feeling proud and superior about our success. This is an auspicious time to chant a few rounds of *Estaghfirullah*.

BEING
IN THE
MYSTERY

"Praise Be to Allah ... Who Made the Angels Messengers with Wings"

(QUR'AN 35:1)

OURS IS A UNIVERSE OF ASTONISHING MYSTERY. ACCORD-
ing to the Qur'an, our planet is visited and populated by all kinds of
invisible energies—angels, *jinn*, and the "slinking whisperer"—who
have been with us since the beginning of Creation. If we think of
ourselves as too sophisticated to believe in such superstitions, Rumi
advises us, "Sell your cleverness and buy bewilderment!" God creates
"as He pleases," says the Qur'an in a verse celebrating both visible
and invisible creation: "Praise be to Allah, Who created out of nothing the Heavens and the Earth, Who made the angels messengers
with wings" (35:1). It is righteousness and an article of Islamic faith
to believe in these genderless, luminous, and invisible beings who act
as intermediaries between God and humanity.

Just as we humans may be said to range in ranks according to
our devotion and surrender to God, the angels are "verily ranged
in ranks [for service]" (37:165). Top-ranked, and usually honored
with the phrase "Upon him be peace" whenever they are mentioned,

are the angels known as Gabriel (*Jibrail*), Michael (*Mika'ail*), Azrael (*Isra'il*), and Raphael (*Israf'il*). The angel Gabriel is entrusted with transmitting divine revelations to all prophets in history, including the Prophet Muhammad during the Night of Power. He also accompanied the Prophet on his night journey and announced to Mary that she would be the virgin mother of Jesus. The angel Michael is responsible for providing sustenance to nurture humanity and knowledge for souls. The angel Azrael, the "angel of death," gathers souls to be returned to God. The angel Raphael will sound the trumpet on the Day of Judgment, "when all that are in the Heavens and on Earth will swoon" (39:68).

The Qur'an mentions hosts of unnamed angels who "celebrate His praises night and day" (21:20), who "sustain the Throne of God" (40:7), and who "celebrate the Praises of their Lord, and pray for forgiveness for [all] beings on Earth" (42:5). Two important angels are *Ridwan* (meaning "good pleasure"), the guardian of Paradise, and *Malik* ("master"), the overseer of Hell. A hadith mentions two additional angels, *Nakir* and *Munkar,* who harshly question the dead in their graves about their faith and good works. Sufi teachers question the authenticity of this hadith, but they tell an amusing story about the Mulla, who instructed his relatives to bury him in an old grave "because when *Munkar* and *Nakir* come, I'll be able to wave them on, saying that this grave has been counted and entered for punishment already."

There is a mystifying account of two angels named *Harut* and *Marut* who were somehow caught up in esoteric knowledge in Babylon, the ancient center of astronomy and other sciences (2:102). Theologians disagree on what actually happened, but one legend has it that angels in Heaven complained to God about the inequities that humans committed on Earth and God replied that if angels possessed free will as humans did, they also would succumb to earthly temptations. The angels chose two of their best members, *Harut* and *Marut,* and God sent them down to Earth endowed with free will. Eventually, *Harut* and *Marut* became corrupted and committed grave sins. Chastened by the experience of *Harut* and *Marut*, angels have been asking God to forgive humanity ever since because they realize that free will is an awesome and burdensome responsibility. An alternative interpretation offered by the respected commentator Yusuf Ali is that *Harut* and *Marut* were not angels at all, but angelically good humans who lived in Babylon and unknowingly imparted esoteric knowledge to ill-intentioned men who used it fraudulently for evil purposes. The lesson in this interpretation is that we have a moral responsibility to pursue and use knowledge wisely and responsibly.

The Qur'an contains numerous revelations about the countless angels who bless us, watch over us, and nudge us toward wise and responsible choices. Each of us has a "protector" (86:4) and angels "before and behind" to guard and to guide in the lifelong work to "change what is within [our]selves" (13:11) and to record our deeds, good or bad (50:17–18, 82:10–12). The Prophet added, "They mind your works: when a work is good, they praise God, and when one is evil, they ask God to forgive you."[1]

Muhammad told his daughter Fatima and her husband, Hazrat Ali, that one of the best spiritual practices he could share with them was a mantra that he learned from the angel Gabriel: *Subhan Allah, Al-hamdulillah, Allahu Akbar*—Glory be to God, Praise be to God, God is Incomparably Great. When we praise and thank God with all our hearts we join a resounding chorus of invisible beings aligned in a powerful vibration and connection with our incomparable Creator. Similarly, we can join with the angels who pray for our forgiveness by praying sincerely for God to forgive those who have wounded or disappointed us. The Qur'anic verse at the beginning of this chapter, "Praise be to Allah ... Who made the angels messengers with wings," goes on to say that those wings number two, three, or even four pairs (35:1). In Islamic spirituality wings are a symbol of soul tenderness. If we humans join our prayers to forgive those who have wronged us with the angelic prayers for humankind, we too shall develop metaphorical wings that will lift us above our burdens of anger and pain.

Jinn

One of the more exotic kinds of invisible beings familiar to readers of Middle Eastern literature such as *Arabian Nights* is the cast of *jinn* (known in English as genies), which predate human beings and were created from the "fire of a scorching wind" (15:27). Like the angels and humans, they were created to worship God. Also like us humans, they possess free will, receive the same Prophetic instructions, and will be held accountable on the Day of Judgment. These beings live among us and can see us even though we cannot see them. According to traditional stories, the *jinn* have their own hierarchies, assemblies, courts of law, weddings, and mourning rituals. As one would expect of beings created from fire and wind, they can travel long distances at great speed. An entire chapter of the Qur'an is devoted to the *jinn*, and there we learn that they can incline, again like humans, toward good or evil: "There are among us some who are righteous, and some the contrary: we follow divergent paths" (72:11). Many of the *jinn* support humans in their noble endeavors in ways we do not understand, while others join Satan in misleading humans and separating them from God. Solomon, who possessed insights into the invisible world, used the services of both humans and *jinn* (27:17). Many healers in the Muslim world, especially in villages, claim to have taught Qur'anic verses to the local *jinn* because the Qur'an says they love to hear "a wondrous discourse guiding toward consciousness of what is right" (72:1). These healers have successfully sought assistance of the *jinn* in the work of healing humans.

Iblis/Shaitan—The Slinking Whisperer

Muslims, like many Christians, believe in a fallen angel, a glorious being that was so impressed with its own magnificence that it clashed with divine will and was banished to hell for its arrogant disobedience. In Islam that angel is called *Iblis* ("the disappointed"), *Shaitan* ("one who is far from God"), and the "slinking whisperer." The sin for which he was banished was his refusal to honor the command that he bow to Allah's beautiful new creation, the human being. "I am better than he," said *Iblis,* whereupon God responded, "Thou art of the meanest of creatures" (7:13), and that was the end of his glory. In a final shout of rebellion, *Iblis* promised to do everything he could to tempt us humans and prove how unworthy we are of our Creator's love and esteem (7:17).

Islamic sages make three points with regard to *Iblis/Shaitan.* First, he was not out of line in questioning the need to bow to us humans, because all creatures are commanded to bow only to God. Rather, the grave error in his disobedience was his unremitting pride and arrogance. Adam and Eve also disobeyed Divinity but they felt contrition and begged forgiveness. The lesson here is that the greatest cause of downfall for human, *jinn,* or angel is arrogance and pride. Second, the energies of the slinking whisperer are not outside of us but in our hearts. Many pilgrims on Hajj throw themselves into a frenzy as they perform the ritual of hurling pebbles at a symbol of the devil in Mina, the place where the devil tempted the prophet Abraham. But of what use is it to curse the devil outside of us when we do little to guard ourselves against the temptations of the slinking whisperer inside our hearts? The Qur'an places responsibility squarely where it belongs: "*Shaitan* caused them to stumble only by means of something they [themselves] had done" (3:155). The third insight is the bewildering paradox that even though God allows *Shaitan* to tempt humans into wrongdoing, God does not approve of his actions. How does one reconcile this conundrum? Rumi asks us to reflect on the following: A doctor needs people to fall sick in order to maintain his or her livelihood. Does this mean that the doctor approves of disease and sickness? Similarly, a baker needs people to be hungry in order to support the business. Does the baker approve of people starving?

Just so, we need temptations in order to flex our spiritual muscles, but that doesn't mean God enjoys watching us struggle. No matter how we humans struggle with our understanding of Satan, Rabia's insight is valuable. When asked if she hated Satan, she replied, "No." The questioner was surprised and asked why not. Rabia answered, "My love for God leaves no room for hating."[2]

REFLECTIONS

Have you ever had an experience with an angel, a *jinn*, or the energies of Satan? If so, in what ways did the encounter impact you and your life?

PRACTICE

Create a cocoon of sacred light to protect you spiritually from harmful forces. Focusing lovingly on divine Heart in your human heart, intend to bring out a golden cord filled with the light of divine protection, and weave the light around you like a gossamer cocoon. The light you weave around you will connect you to the light of angels. The Qur'an says, "I shall, verily, aid you with a thousand angels, following one upon another" (8:9).

"What Is This Love and Laughter?"

(HAFIZ)

ALL MY TEACHERS HAVE TAUGHT ME THAT AN AWAK-
ened soul is filled not only with wisdom but also with love and laughter. The best learning, they say, comes from listening to those whose
souls have truly awakened and are preparing for the journey Home. Indeed, my greatest learning has come from listening to friends who were
diagnosed with terminal illnesses and were preparing for the sacred but
bewildering journey to the other side. We had shared good times and
difficulties for many years, but our friendship deepened immeasurably
as their death approached and many barriers of the ego collapsed to reveal their most authentic selves. From that beautiful, vulnerable center
they graciously shared a few final, precious insights—not with somber
solemnity, as one might expect, but with the sweetness and gentle
humor of a soul that was already beginning to experience a delicious
lightness, free of the burdens of physical and psychological concerns.
The sage Hafiz asks, "What is this love and laughter bubbling up from
within me?" The reply: "It's the sound of a soul waking up!"

The awakened soul of Abdi Sami, who appears earlier in this
book, knew that our lives circle around love: The dramas and

melodramas are all about being loved, not being loved, and wanting to be loved. How little we know about love! Twice divorced, Abdi fully understood Rumi's insight that too often we experience love as subtle degrees of domination and servitude. But this is not love! Love arrives complete like the Moon in the sky; like an ocean whose depth cannot be fathomed. One of Abdi's favorite Qur'anic verses was "We are closer to you than your jugular vein" (50:16). The ultimate Beloved and Source of Love is God. But loving God with all our being requires that we continuously deepen and expand our inner capacity to love ourselves and others more and more, again and again. Never give up on love! With the barrier of his ego collapsed, Abdi was ecstatic about the discovery of boundless love within him and unabashedly shared affection with visitors, friends, and loved ones. Referring to a Rumi poem, Abdi's dying wish was to become a "love dog." In the poem a pious man whose lips grew sweet with longing as he cried "Allah! Allah!" was asked by a cynic if he ever received a return message. The question pierced his heart and he stopped praying. Later, in a vision, the voice of Khidr explained, "The deep longing you express *is* the return message." He asked if he had ever listened to the moan of a dog for its master. That whining is the connection! Khidr continued that there are love dogs no one knows the names of, and advised, "Give your life to be one of them." Love dog Abdi Sami passed away in June 2012, held and embraced by his dearest friends.

Linda Jo, a dear friend for two decades, lived a holistic lifestyle and was surprised to learn that her liver was severely damaged. Through the help of dedicated friends who rallied and advocated for her, she received a liver transplant just in time. But after a few short years she learned that she had terminal brain cancer. A committed theosophist with a deeply intellectual mind, she was puzzled at first and dejected by this new diagnosis. But as she reflected on the subtle mysteries of karma, she found laughter and joy in the insight that cause and effect are not always linear. What we do today may not be the cause but the effect of what we do tomorrow. Somehow that higher understanding brought her inner peace. Linda Jo loved Mulla stories and was especially delighted by one that supported the insight about the nonlinear nature of cause and effect.

The Mulla visited a city bathhouse dressed in peasant garb and received scant care and attention from the two attendants. As he left, the Mulla offered both attendants a gold coin, and they were stunned and chagrined at having ignored a wealthy client. The Mulla returned the following week, and this time the attendants lavished attention on him, offering him the best of soaps, perfumes, and massages. As the Mulla left, he offered each of them a measly copper coin, saying, "These copper coins are for last time, and the gold coins given last week are for this time!"

When the doctors finally told Linda Jo that there was nothing more that medical science could do for her, she confided that this was the first time she was not able to be in control of her life, and she felt confused. We talked at length about the meaning of surrender. Two days before she died, as she lay on her hospice bed, she looked so alert and healthy, but so determined to surrender, that we both burst out laughing. I talked and talked about surrender, but Linda Jo gently focused attention on her heart and lovingly and repeatedly said to it, "I surrender to you." Linda Jo's surrender of her body and soul to her Creator was especially tender.

When my beloved cousin Ghulam Mustafa finally accepted and came to terms with the fact that he was dying of lung cancer, he took refuge in the cycles of body prayers and the Qur'an. But what truly stirred and awakened his soul was listening to his favorite Bengali songs and music. It was as if, by listening to these magical sounds, some vague heavenly memories were becoming clearer and he was remembering a previous life in God's embrace. He laughed gently and shook his head in disbelief that his conservative friends could say any singing other than holy recitals is sacrilegious. During a celebration of his life a few days before he died, I told him Rumi's story about a conservative Muslim who complained during an all-night session of songs and music in praise of God, "What is all this music, music, music?" Rumi replied that music is the "sound of the creaking of the doors of Paradise." The man replied that he hated the sound of creaking! Retorted Rumi, "That's because when you hear the creaking, for you the doors of Paradise are closing!" Weak as he was, Mustafa managed a broad smile and a deep chuckle at Rumi's words. Mustafa loved the insight of the great Islamic sage Al-Ghazzali that if listening to songs is forbidden by conservative Muslims, then the beautiful chirping of birds and the sounds of Allah's other creatures should also be prohibited. As per my cousin's wishes, we celebrated Ghulam Mustafa's life over food, song, and music before and after he died. The celebration continues every year on the anniversary of his return Home.

I mentioned in a previous chapter my elegant, witty, and globe-trotting friend Janet Turner. When she was told that her life span might be limited to five to seven years because of a kidney condition, she felt an awakening and a longing to be free of the constraints she had imposed on her life by always seeking approval from others. One day Janet heard me cite the saying from Taoism and Sufism, "Whoever's approval you seek, you become prisoner, so choose your jailors with care and deliberation," and was so deeply moved that she made changes in her relationships and priorities and committed her life to Spirit and Love. About a year later, she took to heart another insight: Blessed are the flexible for they will never be bent out of shape. She was in the process of healing broken relationships and the insight freed her to make compromises and shifts. The last time I heard her playful voice on the phone, she wanted to discuss a poem and riddle by the twelfth-century Sufi master Fariduddin Attar: "Street-sweeper, something about you bothers me. You walk the streets looking for something you haven't lost. You can never find it!" Replies the street-sweeper, "And even stranger, if I do not find what I have not lost, I get frantic with worry."[1] A few weeks before she died, Janet laughed and said that Spirit might mercifully give her an extension of life because she had not found what she had not lost—but just in case that was not to be, she was flexible and would not be bent out of shape! When she died, Janet was drained of color but there was a distinctive expression on her face. In it were grace, beauty, and the subtle hint of a playful smile.

I was privileged to be a spiritual companion to my friend Rich Henry during his final days. He and his wife, Ruth Ann, are founders of a church called Unity Peace Center of Woodinville, Washington. They are two of the most pious, devoted, and humble servants of God I know. In his gentle voice, Rich Henry struggled to find words to express the joy he felt about the oneness of everything and everybody that he was experiencing. We talked about religion and agreed with Rumi's insight that what is praised is One, so the praise is also one. All religions and all this singing are really one song. There is the imagery of many jugs of water being poured into a huge basin. The differences are just illusion and vanity. Rich Henry smiled and repeated, "It's all One." In a way, there was nothing new that I heard as I spent these last precious hours with Rich, but the deep source from which he drew his words imparted an astonishing freshness to the insights. Even more, the unconditional love evident in Rich's eyes and his celestial smile stirred my own soul and moved me to tears. I realized that I could not fathom even a fraction of Rich Henry's awareness of oneness, now that his soul was awakening and preparing to become one with the One.

REFLECTIONS

Spiritual teachers point out that after you die, from the other side you will reflect upon your dramas and melodramas on

Earth, and will laugh and laugh! The same teachers ask, "Why not laugh now?"

What are some dramatic situations in your life that you can laugh about now?

PRACTICE

The physical and spiritual benefits of laughter are amazing! Make it a regular spiritual practice to laugh in community. Gather together with good friends, fling out your arms, and simply start to laugh, even if you have to force it. You will be surprised by how infectious laughter is! Check out the global "laughter club" movement, which originated in India: www. laughteryoga.org.

GEM 32

"To God We Belong and to God We Are Returning"

(QUR'AN 2:156)

RABIA, THE NINTH-CENTURY SUFI SAGE FAMED FOR THE ardor and exuberance of her love for God, was seen rushing through the streets with a pail of water and a torch of fire, declaring to all she met that she wanted to quench the fires of Hell and set fire to Heaven. Would that we could muster a fraction of Rabia's wild enthusiasm in our service of the Beloved! Well, could we pause for a moment and reflect on our motives for trying to live a godly life? Are we acting out of sheer love of God or are we motivated by a fear of Hell or expectation of Heaven? Allowing our spiritual life to be motivated by either aversion or greed leads to serious deformity, as illustrated by a Sufi story in which the prophet Jesus came across two groups of people bent over and disabled with worry and anxieties. One group was terrified of the scorching fires of Hell, while the other was frantic with desire to enjoy the sensual pleasures of Heaven. Both motivations are unworthy, say the sages. May we take Rabia's famous prayer to heart: "O Allah! If I worship You for fear of Hell, burn me in Hell. And if I worship You in hope of Paradise, exclude me from Paradise. But if I worship You for Your own sake, grudge me not your Everlasting Beauty."[1]

Heaven and Hell

The Qur'an describes Heaven in exquisitely sensual details as a place of "gardens under which rivers flow" and "beautiful mansions in gardens of everlasting bliss" (9:72) where abound "companions, with beautiful, big, and lustrous eyes" (44:54), "immortal youths" (56:17), and "all that your souls shall desire" (41:31). Now the Qur'an itself tells us that some of its passages are meant to be taken literally and others metaphorically (3:7)—though it does not tell us which is which—so it might be a mistake to count on a Heaven filled with mansions and alluring companions. Spiritual commentators point out that the Qur'an's descriptions of Heaven would have had great appeal to the seventh-century audience it was trying to reform. Luxuriant gardens with flowing streams would resonate with people of the arid desert, and the description of fair virgins with lustrous eyes spoke to the desires and fantasies of the Arab men of that time.

By the same token, descriptions of Hell as an "evil destination" (48:6), a "bottomless pit" (101:9) filled with "a fierce blast of fire and ... boiling water ... and black smoke" (56:42–43) wherein anguished souls heave with sighs and sobs (11:106) were meant to dissuade seventh-century Arab tribesmen from reckless savagery and a hedonistic lifestyle. Their lack of morals stemmed from a belief that there is nothing in life but this world (45:24), says the Qur'an, and they scoffed at the idea of accountability in the Other World as "but tales of the ancients" (23:81). Thus the Qur'an makes of the Day of Judgment a momentous theme and of Hell a frightening place.

Whether to downplay the literal import of its physical descriptions of Heaven or to hint that they are allegorical, the Qur'an tells us that even in "gardens of everlasting bliss," the greatest bliss is "the Good Pleasure of God." "That," says the Qur'an, "is the supreme felicity" (9:72). No matter how delightful the eternal pleasures of Heaven may be, measured by our earthly knowledge, our souls yearn for the singular fulfillment that comes from proximity to God. Similarly, many spiritual teachers say the true cause of misery in Hell is the soul's separation from God. Sufi teachers believe that Hell is less a place of punishment and more a place of purification, a temporary stop on the way to becoming whole. In a poignant verse, the Qur'an says that for those who have too few good deeds, Hell will be their "mother" (101:9), suggesting that Hell is a womb of divine mercy where those who have not done their inner work get a second chance at development and purification before being delivered anew to continue their mysterious journey into further realms. The Prophet Muhammad said, "Allah will command, 'Bring out of the fire anyone in whose heart there is faith or goodness, even to the extent of a mustard seed.'"

Spiritual Perspective

In Islamic spirituality, Heaven and Hell are way stations as we continue our journey toward union with God. On Judgment Day, "sharp is thy sight" (50:22) and anyone who has done "an atom's weight of good or evil" shall see it clearly (99:7–8). We shall become fully aware of where we followed the righteous path and where we strayed. Based on our level of attainment on Earth, we shall be placed in one of the levels of Heaven and we shall continue to evolve into perfection and spiral into higher and higher states of unity with Divinity. God, Who is "the Creator, Evolver, the Bestower of Forms" (59:24) and "Lord of the Ways of Ascent" (70:3), will transform us into beings whose forms we can't currently imagine (56:61). Rumi says that as we pass from our human form, we shall assume an angelic soul and move into states that our minds cannot even conceive. We shall experience reincarnation not on Earth but in the exalted levels of Heaven.

The essential point of the Qur'anic revelations about the afterlife is that while they are directed to the part of our ego nature that is motivated by desire for Heaven and fear of Hell—they also call us to transcend our basic ego nature and climb the ladder of enlightenment. No living human knows for sure whether Heaven and Hell are physical places or spiritual states of being. But what we can take on certain faith, and live accordingly, is a beautiful Qur'anic verse: "To

God we belong and to God we are returning" (2:156). That home-coming will be supreme felicity indeed.

REFLECTIONS

The Prophet and his companions were talking about the fires of Hell when they chanced to see a woman running frantically to and fro in search of her missing child. When she found the child, she cradled and suckled it with such gratitude, love, and care that the companions wept. Said the Prophet to his companions, "Do you think this mother could ever throw her child into the fire?" The companions replied, "How could that be possible?!" "Even more than this woman loves her child does God love His servants," the Prophet remarked.

What are your personal beliefs about Heaven and Hell? How do they guide your actions?

PRACTICE

Meditate on Rumi's utterance, which might also refer to the afterlife:

> Out beyond ideas of wrongdoing and right doing there
> is a field. I'll meet you there.
>
> RUMI

"A Lovesick Nightingale among Owls"

(RUMI)

WE ALL KNOW THE WITTY TRUISM THAT THE PRIMARY cause of death is being born, but most of us ignore or even deny that inconvenient truth for most of our lives. We go for years on end dreaming and scheming about ways to improve our lives here on Earth, with little thought to preparing our souls for the afterlife. As the Sufi sage Al-Ghazzali remarked, "You make clothes for winter but no provision for another life."[1] Muhammad's son-in-law, Hazrat Ali, noted, "Everyone who is being overtaken by death asks for more time, while everyone who still has time makes excuses for procrastination."[2] It's later than we think, as the Mulla tried to explain to a guide in the London Museum. Hearing the guide remark that an artifact was five thousand years old, the Mulla stepped forward to offer a correction: "Five thousand and four years old." The guide ignored him and turned to another artifact, announcing that it was two thousand years old. Again the Mullah corrected the guide: "Two thousand and four years old." Now the guide was visibly annoyed. In a sharp tone he said, "Sir, I can see that you come from the mysterious East, but how can you be so sure about the precise dates?" "Simple," replied the Mulla. "I was here four years ago and those are the dates you mentioned then!"

The Qur'an also warns us about the swift passing of time. Be mindful of God "with all the mindfulness that is due Him," it urges, and "do not allow death to overtake you before you have surrendered yourselves to Him" (3:102). In Islamic spirituality, as in Judaism, we experience a form of little death every day when our souls ascend into the embrace of God while we sleep. When we awaken, says the Qur'an, God sends our souls back into our bodies "for a term appointed" (39:42). Aside from these mini experiences of death, we also taste death in many different forms: the death of hopes and dreams, the ending of relationships, the physical death of loved ones. It is a beautiful spiritual practice to give ourselves permission to experience the feelings of loss and sadness that accompany these deaths, for the sages say that the more our sad feelings carve into our being, the more joy we can contain. This doesn't mean we should run toward feelings of sadness, only that we shouldn't run away from them.

Spiritual Practices and Insights

Another truism is that the real reason we avoid thinking about death is that we are afraid not of dying, but of failing to be fully alive. Favored Sufi practices include visiting the terminally ill, attending their funerals, participating in rituals to honor the dead, and even visiting the occasional graveyard. These practices not only help us overcome our fear of death, but also heighten our awareness of the transitory nature of life so that we may live our remaining years with greater clarity and intention. When imbued with the consciousness of our inevitable death, we realize at a heart level that time is precious and we no longer want to waste energy enmeshed in trivialities and distractions. Priorities and plans seem to rearrange themselves almost of their own accord. We resonate with the wisdom of the Bengali poet Tagore: "We spend our days and nights stringing and unstringing our instruments, but the song we came here to sing remains unsung."[3]

In my interfaith congregation we make a conscious effort to gather together after a member has died, not only to honor our friend but also to share thoughts and feelings about our own eventual demise. Our senior members have much to teach about learning to accept and embrace this stage of life graciously and gracefully, rather than evading it with worldly distractions. This is one of the many blessings of a community of faith: The company of close friends makes it much easier to face our fears with courage and an open heart. When friends allow themselves to be vulnerable and share their fears about old age and death, almost invariably the fears give way to insight and tears turn to laughter. The Hindu sage Ramama Maharshi says that when we die and look back on our earthly life, at our dramas and melodramas, we shall laugh and laugh. So why not laugh right now while we are alive on Earth?!

This being a spiritual community, we naturally end up putting a spiritual spin on the physical ailments that concern us. If my eyes are failing, Sufi wisdom teaches, it's because my soul has wept so copiously with longing for God that my sight has become cloudy and dim. If my spine is bent and sore, that's because it has borne the burden of my soul's grief at being parted from God. After sharing a few such insights, we are all in a better humor about our various frailties, and soon we are offering to support each other as best we can, like the strong-legged blind man and his lame-but-sighted friend helping each other get to the king's banquet (Gem 20).

In the midst of our celebration and laughter, we also talk candidly about serious theological issues. At least three friends in our community have committed suicide and two have passed away by choosing "death with dignity." Suicide is not condoned in Islam—it is not condoned in most other religions, either—but as we refer to sacred verses that reflect our personal opinions and pull us in different directions, we quickly realize that any human judgment feels sacrilegious, self-righteous, and superfluous. What feels sacred, loving, and fulfilling is to send love and prayers to the departed souls and humbly serve the All-Merciful God by providing sincere support and consolation to the surviving family members.

Almost invariably, as our conversations turn to preparations for our own death, my companions ask for insights that might be gleaned from the Prophet Muhammad's final days. The first insight I always mention is that one of Muhammad's last acts was to spend hours in a graveyard meditating and praying for the souls of the departed, even though he himself was in feeble health. This had been an integral part of his spiritual practice throughout his life, and he continued it right up to death's door. Friends who engage in this practice report that these sacred visits give urgency and meaning to their lives and slowly usher their minds and hearts into the deathless state. In this state, one is freed from fear of dying and realizes that this passage is simply another stage in the journey toward union with God. A second insight is that the Prophet humbly sought to make amends for any wrongs and repay any debts before he died. Three days before his death, during his last attendance at the mosque, he asked once again whether he owed anyone money or an apology. This time a man rose and claimed three dirhams (a unit of currency), which he had given to a poor man at the behest of the Prophet. Muhammad promptly repaid the man and explained his attempts to discharge his debts with the famous words, "It is better to blush in this world than in the next."[4] At least three friends have told me in their dying days that this utterance moved them to discharge their debts and make amends with loved ones and enemies with urgency and sacredness. The third insight also arises from his last attendance at his mosque. Turning to his daughter, Fatima, and his aunt, Safiya, he said, "Do ye works that will please Thy Sustainer." What better advice could we seek from our beloved Prophet, whose own lips uttered the revelation, "To God we belong and to God is our return" (2:156). All we can offer our Creator when we return Home is a sound heart and righteous deeds.

Ultimate Surrender and Day of Resurrection

Death is our ultimate surrender as we participate in the sacred process of releasing our soul from the cage of our body. The Qur'an says we have no idea what joy the soul feels in returning to the embrace of God. "O soul in complete rest and satisfaction!" says the Holy Book. "Return to your Sustainer well-pleased and well-pleasing!" (89:27–28). That returning soul is exemplified by the most poetic of birds in Rumi's well-loved verse, "A love-sick nightingale among owls, you caught the scent of roses and flew to the Rose garden."[5]

Muslims believe that the soul has a joyful reunion with its Creator and is then placed in a mysterious state of quiescence called *barzakh* (23:100) to await the Day of Resurrection. Preceding the Day of Resurrection, also known as the Day of Judgment or the Day of the Gathering, there will be an era of tumultuous instability on Earth. According to the Qur'an, the prophet Jesus, whom God had raised up "unto Himself" (4:158), will return to Earth to establish a period of peace and equity. Soon after that, the Earth will be visited by a series of cataclysmic events, "when the sky is cleft asunder; when the stars are scattered; when the oceans are suffered to burst forth; and when the graves are turned upside down" (82:1–4) and the dead will be called to acknowledge "what has seduced thee from Thy Lord Most Beneficent" (82:6). The Qur'an says that on that fateful day, when "sharp is thy sight" (50:22), we will have no choice but to lay bare the truth (69:1) and our bodies will testify against us about any wrongs we have done. Rumi surmises that our hands might say, "I stole money"; our lips, "I said meanness"; our feet, "I went where I shouldn't"; and our genitals, "Me, too!" According to tradition, we shall be called to account for four questions: how we spent our life on Earth, how we utilized our knowledge, how we acquired and spent our wealth, and how we wore out our body. When the accounting in the presence of angels and the divine Judge is complete, the righteous "will be in Bliss" and the wicked "will be in the Fire" (82:13–14).

As noted earlier (Gem 32), no one knows whether these descriptions of the afterlife are literal or metaphorical. The Mulla does not want to take any chances. He instructs his wife and family not to place any headstone over his grave when he dies. When asked why, he replies, "On the Day of Judgment, when I arise from my grave, I don't want my head to bang against the headstone. I want to be clearheaded!"

Over the centuries, deeply enlightened Sufi teachers have smiled at the incongruous image of our All-Merciful Sustainer sitting in punitive judgment over the humans He created with such love, and asking what we've done when He already knows our every deed. On the Day of Gathering, these teachers laughingly say, they will make two requests of God: "Plead and advocate on my behalf with Yourself!" and "Do what is worthy of Thee and not me!"

REFLECTIONS

Originator of the Heavens and the Earth! Thou art near unto me in this world and in the life to come: Let me die as one who has surrendered himself unto Thee, and make me one with the righteous.

QUR'AN 12:101

The grave is the first stage of the journey into Eternity.[6]

HADITH

When we are dead, seek not our tomb in the Earth, but find it in the hearts of men.

EPITAPH ON RUMI'S GRAVE

What epitaph would you like to be inscribed on your grave?

PRACTICE

From time to time, as an integral part of your spiritual practice, meditate on your death. Aware of the mystery of death, meditate on the Prophet's words, "It is better to blush in this world than in the next." Ask yourself what you might do to purify your heart more deeply, say what needs to be said to others, and perform more righteous deeds. Do all of this not with a sense of fear but out of a soul-felt desire to become free and fulfilled. The Prophet has sage advice for all of us: "When you were born, everyone was smiling but you were crying. Live such a life that when you depart, everyone is weeping but you are smiling."

ACKNOWLEDGMENTS

I wish to express profound gratitude to my extended family for the blessings of their unbounded love and support : daughter Kristina, sister Aysu, brother Kamal and my close relatives Naz, Diran, Neal, Esha, Emana, Ataur, Suraiya, Javed , Ummul, Nuzhat, Sufiara, Ismet, Ishtiaque, Ripa, Tanvir and Ashu.

Heart-felt thanks to my life-long and deeply cherished friends Karen Lindquist, Sally Jo De Vargas, Katayoon Naficy and Faren Bachelis. Their dedication to truth and service are a source of deep inspiration and learning for me.

Abundant thanks to an esteemed family friend, Kate Elias. Most graciously and generously she shared her prodigious talents of editing and scholarship in the shaping of this book. I am truly indebted to her.

I am blessed by the friendship and wisdom of my Interfaith Amigos Rabbi Ted Falcon and Pastor Donald Mackenzie. I am beholden to my circle of friends from classes and Interfaith Community Sanctuary. They persist in doing the inconvenient inner work of transforming ego and opening the heart with humility and sincerity. Through their example, I strive to become a better Muslim and a more complete human being.

I am very thankful to the devoutly Christian proprietors and employees of Grumpy D, a local coffee house where I did my writing.

They constantly offered me hospitality, support and enthusiasm for "the Muslim book."

I am highly grateful to Emily Wichland, vice president of Editorial and Production at SkyLight Paths Publishing for her abiding encouragement, support, and expertise. Many thanks also to Kaitlin Johnstone, assistant editor.

NOTES

Introduction

1. Imagery borrowed from Rumi's poetry.
2. The Kabah is a large stone structure, draped in black cloth, which stands in the center of the Grand Mosque in Mecca. According to tradition, the foundation was laid by Adam and the building constructed by Abraham and Ishmael. The Kabah establishes the direction of prayer for all Muslims around the world.

GEM 1: "This Is the Book" (Qur'an 2:2)—"Meditate on Its Signs" (Qur'an 38:29)

1. Rafiq Zakaria, *Muhammad and the Quran* (London: Penguin Books, 1991), 64.
2. Ibid., 12.
3. Zafar Khan, ed., "The Standard of Hadith Criticism," from Muhammad H. Haykal, *The Life of Muhammad* (Baltimore: American Trust Publications, 2005), www.islamawareness.net/Hadith/hadith_criticisms.html (accessed January 13, 2013).

GEM 2: "The Qur'an Is a Shy and Veiled Bride" (Rumi)

1. Rumi's quatrain No. 1173 (38) in *Divan-e-Shams-e-Tabriz.*

GEM 3: "I Was a Secret Treasure and I Longed to Be Known" (Hadith Qudsi)

1. In Sufi symbolism, wine is divine knowledge that intoxicates the soul, and a tavern is a gathering place of Sufis.
2. Javad Nurbakhsh, *Traditions of the Prophet* (New York: Khaniqahi Nimatul-lahi Publications, 1981), 13, 56.

GEM 4: "We Have Not Known You as We Should Have" (Hadith)

1. Llewellyn Vaughan-Lee, *Travelling the Path of Love: Sayings of Sufi Masters* (San Francisco: The Golden Sufi Center, 1994), 180.

2. Unauthenticated but extensively used by Sufi teachers based on Qur'an 50:22 and 53:57–58, to explain the spiritual concept of *kashf*, or unveiling.

GEM 5: "Know Thyself and You Shall Know Thy Lord" (Hadith)

1. Unauthenticated but popularly used by sages and laypeople, for example, it appears in contemporary spiritual writer Kabir Helminski's book *The Knowing Heart: A Sufi Path of Transformation* (Boston and London: Shambhala Publications, Inc., 1999).

2. Vaughan-Lee, *Travelling the Path of Love*, 216.

3. Dr. N. K. Singh, *Global Encyclopedia of Islamic Mystics and Mysticism* (New Delhi: Global Vision Publishing House, 2004), 50.

4. This hadith is expounded upon by a famous ninth-century Persian scholar and mystic, Sahlal-Tustari, in *The New Encyclopedia of Islam* by Cyril Glasse (Lanham, MD: Rowan & Littlefield Publishers, Inc., 2008), 393.

GEM 6: "Die Before You Die" (Hadith)

1. Popular hadith related by one of the greatest scholars of Islam, Ibn Arabi (d. 1240), and used extensively in Islamic spiritual literature.

2. James Turner Johnson, *The Holy War in Western and Islamic Traditions* (Philadelphia: University of Pennsylvania Press, 2002), 35.

GEM 7: "The Road Is Long, the Sea Is Deep" (Fariduddin Attar)

1. All the quotations in this chapter are from Peter Sis, *The Conference of the Birds* (New York: Penguin Press, 2001).

GEM 9: "We Have Made Some of You as a Trial for Others: Will You Have Patience?" (Qur'an 25:20)

1. Aleksandr I. Solzhenitsyn, *The Gulag Archipelago: An Experiment in Literary Investigation*, 1918–1956 (New York: Basic Books, 1997), 168.

GEM 11: "Will You Not See? Will You Not Listen? Will You Not Pay Attention?" (Qur'an 54:17, 7:204)

1. Rabindranath Tagore, *Stray Birds* (New York: The Macmillan Company, 1916), 6.

GEM 12: "O My Lord! Open for Me My Heart!" (Qur'an 20:25)

1. Vaughan-Lee, *Travelling the Path of Love*, 62.

2. Vaughan-Lee, *Travelling the Path of Love*, 48.

GEM 13: "Bring to God a Sound Heart" (Qur'an 26:89)

1. C. Helminski, *The Book of Character* (Watsonville, CA: The Book Foundation, 2004), 331.

2. "Maxims of the Holy Prophet (S.A.W.) and the Imams (A.S.)," www. imamreza.net/eng/imamreza.php?id=3179 (accessed January 16, 2013).

GEM 17: "Bow in Adoration and Draw Closer" (Qur'an 96:19)

1. C. Helminski, *The Book of Character*, 157.

GEM 20: "Ah! What a Beautiful Fellowship!" (Qur'an 4:69)

1. C. Helminski, *The Book of Character*, 380.
2. As reported by Fariduddin Attar in his thirteenth-century book *Tadhkirat al-Auliya*.

GEM 21: "Be Just; This Is Closest to Being God-Conscious." (Qur'an 5:8)

1. C. Helminski, *The Book of Character*, 59–60.
2. This story was reported in a blog: http://cacoescrib.wordpress. com/2012/03/05/when-justice-is-tempered-with-mercy (accessed January 13, 2013) and in http://www.liveleak.com/view?i=5c1_1331898047; http://bloginfo4uall.blogspot.com/2012/03/wanita-miskin-didenda-rp-1-juta-kerana.html (accessed January 13, 2013).
3. Robert Bly, *The Kabir Book: Forty-four of the Ecstatic Poems of Kabir* (Boston: Beacon Press, 1993), 55.

GEM 25: "Move from Knowledge of the Tongue to Knowledge of the Heart" (Traditional Saying)

1. Charles Le Gai Eaton, *The Book of Hadith: Sayings of the Prophet Muhammad, from the Mishkat al-Masabi* (Watsonville, CA: The Book Foundation, 2008), 79.

GEM 26: "Whoever ... Believes in God Has Grasped the Most Trustworthy Handhold" (Qur'an 2:256)

1. Idries Shah, *Tales of the Dervishes: Teaching-Stories of the Sufi Masters Over the Past Thousand Years* (London: Penguin Books, 1993), 23–24.

GEM 27: "Women Are the Twin-Halves of Men" (Hadith)

1. Kabir Helminski, ed., *The Rumi Collection: An Anthology of Translations of Mevlana Jalaluddin Rumi* (Boston: Shambhala, 1999), 6.

GEM 28: "Come to Know Each Other" (Qur'an 49:13)

1. News report of *Time* poll by Alex Altman, www.time.com/time/nation/article/0,8599,2011799,00.html (accessed January 13, 2013).
2. John L. Esposito and Dalia Mogahed, *Who Speaks for Islam: What a Billion Muslims Really Think* (New York: Gallup Press, 2007), 155.

GEM 29: "Be Quick in the Race for Forgiveness from Your Lord" (Qur'an 3:133)

1. C. Helminski, *The Book of Character*, 50.
2. Ibid., 64.

3. www.bbc.co.uk/news/world-asia-india-18856594 (accessed January 13, 2013).
4. Carl Jung, *Mysterium Cuniunctionis*, 1955–1956, *The Collected Works of CJ Jung*, Vol. 14, trans. G. Adler and R.F.C. Hall (Princeton, NJ: Princeton University Press, 1977).

GEM 30: "Praise Be to Allah ... Who Made the Angels Messengers with Wings" (Qur'an 35:1)

1. Quoted in "The Angels," by Sachiko Murata, www.islamawareness.net/Angels/murata.html (accessed January 13, 2013).
2. Robert Frager and James Fadiman, *Essential Sufism* (San Francisco: HarperCollins, 1997), 119.

GEM 31: "What Is This Love and Laughter?" (Hafiz)

1. Inayat Khan and Coleman Barks, *The Hand of Poetry: Five Mystic Poets of Persia* (New York: Omega Publications, 1993), 56.

GEM 32: "To God We Belong and to God We Are Returning" (Qur'an 2:156)

1. Robert Frager and James Fadiman, *Essential Sufism* (San Francisco: HarperCollins, 1997), 229.

GEM 33: "A Lovesick Nightingale among Owls" (Rumi)

1. Idries Shah, *The Way of the Sufi* (London: Penguin Books, 1974), 62.
2. Thomas Cleary, *Living and Dying with Grace: Counsels of Hazrat Ali* (Boston: Shambhala, 1996), 49.
3. Sarah Lawall, Maynard Mack, et al., eds., *The Norton Anthology of World Literature*, Vol. F (New York: W.W. Norton & Company, 2002), 1674–1675.
4. C. Helminski, *The Book of Character*, 58.
5. James Cowan, *Where Two Oceans Meet: A Selection of Odes from the Divan of Shems of Tabriz* (Rockport, Mass.: Elements Books Ltd., 1992), 101.
6. Al-Mamun Al-Suhrawardy, *The Sayings of Muhammad* (London: Archibald Constable and Co. Ltd., 1905), 18.

SELECTED QUR'ANIC PASSAGES AND HADITH

Remembrance of God/God-Consciousness

... truly, in the remembrance of God hearts find rest. (13:28)

We are nearer to him than his jugular vein. (50:16)

Wherever you turn, there is the Face of Allah. (2:115)

To God belong the most beautiful names. (59:24)

We have bestowed on you the source of abundance. So to your Sustainer turn in prayer and sacrifice. (108:1–2)

God draws to Himself those who are willing, and guides to Himself everyone who turns to Him. (42:13)

If Allah helps you, none can overcome you: If He forsakes you, who is there, after that, that can help you? (3:160)

If one desires the rewards of this world, let him remember that with God are the rewards of both this world and the life to come. (4:134)

And paradise will be brought near to the God-conscious, no longer will it be distant. (50:31)

For the one who remains conscious of God, He always prepares a way of emergence and He provides for him in ways that he could never imagine. (65:2)

Keep your tongue forever moistened with the name of Allah. (HADITH)

If my servant draws near to me a hand span, I draw near to him an arm's length; and if he draws near to me an arm's length, I draw near to him a fathom's length. And if he comes to me walking, I come to him running. (HADITH)

The Signs of Nature

All that is on Earth will perish; but forever will abide the Face of your Sustainer, Full of Majesty and Abundant Honor. (55:26–27)

And He it is who makes the night as a robe for you, and sleep as repose, and makes every day a resurrection. (25:47)

So I call to witness the rosy glow of sunset, the night and its progression and the Moon as it grows into fullness: Surely you shall travel from stage to stage. (84:16–19)

Assuredly, the creation of the Heavens and the Earth is a greater [matter] than the creation of men; yet most people understand not. (40:57)

And do not walk upon the Earth with proud self-conceit; for, truly, you can never rend the Earth asunder, nor can you grow as tall as the mountains! (17:37)

Adore your Guardian Lord … who has made the Earth your couch and the Heavens your canopy; and sent down rain from the Heavens; and brought forth therewith fruits for your sustenance. (2:21–22)

Compassion

In the Name of God, the Infinitely Compassionate, Most Merciful.
(OPENS VIRTUALLY ALL CHAPTERS OF THE QUR'AN)

My Mercy overspreads everything.   (7:156)

When an orphan cries, the throne of God shakes.   (HADITH)

Allah is the Lord of grace abounding.   (2:105)

If kindness were a visible creation, nothing which Allah has created would be more beautiful than it.   (HADITH)

Inner Work

Truly my prayer, and all my acts of worship, and my living and my dying are for God alone, the Sustainer of all worlds. (6:162)

This Book of Blessings We have sent down to you—so that they may meditate upon its signs, and that people of insight might take them to heart.   (38:29)

Die before you die.   (HADITH)

Know thyself and you shall know thy Sustainer.   (HADITH)

Worship as if you can see God, and if you cannot see God, know that God sees you.   (HADITH)

Spacious Heart

O my Sustainer! Open up my heart [to Thy light].   (20:25)

Even if the religious judge advises you about worldly affairs, first consult your heart.   (HADITH)

Verily, God does not change men's condition unless they change their inner selves.   (13:11)

Neither my Heaven nor my Earth can contain me, but the soft, humble heart of my believing slave can contain me.   (HADITH)

God has made the Earth a wide expanse for you, so that you might walk thereon on spacious paths.   (71:20)

Divine Qualities: Patience, Sincerity, Humility, Truth

We have made some of you as a trial for others. Will ye have patience?   (25:20)

The sincere servants of God, for them is an appointed nourishment—fruits, and honor, and dignity, in gardens of felicity ...
(37:40–43)

Bow down in adoration and draw near!   (96:19)

Are you not aware how God offers the parable of a good word? It is like a good tree, firmly rooted, reaching its branches toward the sky, always yielding fruit, by consent of its Sustainer.   (14:24–25)

Praise and Gratitude

Don't you see that God has made in service to you all that is in the Heavens and on Earth, and has made His bounties flow to you in abundant measure, seen and unseen?   (31:20)

In the abundance of God and in His grace, in that let them rejoice; that is better than whatever they may hoard.   (10:58)

All that is in the Heavens and all that is on Earth extols the limitless glory of God.   (62:1)

That which is from the Presence of God is better than any bargain or passing delight! For God is the best of providers.   (62:11)

Are you not aware that it is God whose limitless glory all creatures in the Heavens and on Earth praise, even the birds as they outspread their wings?   (24:41)

Knowledge

O my Sustainer! Increase my knowing. (20:114)

O God, make me see things as they really are. (HADITH)

The ink of the scholar is more holy than the blood of the martyr.
(HADITH)

You have been granted very little of [real] knowledge. (17:85)

Faith

So truly, with every difficulty comes ease: truly with every difficulty comes ease. So when you are free from your task, continue to strive, and to your Sustainer turn with loving attention.
(94:5–8)

I listen to the prayer of every supplicant when he calleth on Me: Let them also, with a will, listen to My call, and believe in Me.
(2:186)

As for those who have attained faith in Allah and hold fast to Him, He will cause them to enter into His compassion and His abundant blessing, and guide them to Himself in a straight way.
(4:175)

Whoever submits his or her whole self to God and is a doer of good has indeed grasped the most trustworthy handhold; for with God rests the final outcome of all endeavors. (31:22)

Forgiveness

O my servants who have transgressed against their souls! Despair not of the Mercy of Allah: for Allah forgives all sins for He is oft-forgiving, Most Merciful. (39:53)

... if one is patient in adversity and forgives—this, behold, is indeed something to set one's heart upon! (42:43)

Invoke the Mercy of God and as milk returns not to the udder, go not back to your wrongdoing. (HADITH)

Justice

Is it not enough that your Lord is witness to all things? (41:53)

Be just: This is closest to being God-conscious. (5:8)

Do not deprive yourselves of the good things of life, which God has made lawful to you, but do not transgress the bounds of what is right. (5:87)

Do not barter away your bond with God for a trifling gain! (16:95)

Behold! God enjoins justice, and the doing of good, and generosity toward [one's] fellow men. (16:90)

Let there be no compulsion in religion. (2:256)

Community

Truly, by token of time, human beings are in loss except those who have faith and do righteous deeds and encourage each other in the teaching of truth and in patient perseverance. (103:1–3)

Make room for one another in your collective life; do make room; [and in return] God will make room for you [in His grace]. (58:11)

If he makes mention of Me within himself, I make mention of him within myself; and if he makes mention of Me in an assembly, I make mention of him in an assembly better than it. (HADITH)

There is not an animal [that lives] on the Earth, nor a being that flies on its wings, but [forms part of] communities like you. (6:38)

Service/Righteous Deeds

Good deeds, the fruit of which endures forever, are best in the sight of your Sustainer, and yield the best return.   (19:76)

Truly those who have faith and do righteous deeds will the Most Gracious endow with Love.   (19:96)

And the likeness of those who spend their substance, seeking to please Allah and to strengthen their souls, is as a garden, high and fertile.   (2:265)

Truly, the most highly regarded of you in the sight of God is the one who does the most good.   (49:13)

Wealth and children are allurements of the life of this world: But the things that endure, good deeds, are best in the sight of thy Lord.   (18:46)

Who is he that will loan to Allah a beautiful loan? For [Allah] will increase it manifold to His credit, and He will have [besides] a liberal reward.   (57:11)

Do good deeds according to your capacity. God does not grow tired of giving rewards unless you tire of doing good. The good deeds most loved by God are those that are done regularly, even if they are small.   (HADITH)

Women and Marriage

For men and women who surrender themselves to God ... and for men and women who remember God unceasingly, for them God has readied forgiveness, and a supreme recompense. (33:35)

Allah hath promised to believers—men and women—gardens under which rivers flow, to dwell therein, and beautiful mansions in gardens of everlasting bliss. But the greatest bliss is the Good Pleasure of Allah: That is the supreme felicity.   (9:72)

It is God who has created you all out of one soul and out of it brought into being a mate, so that man might incline with love toward woman. (7:189)

God created for you mates from among yourselves that you may dwell in tranquility with them, and He engenders love and compassion between you; truly in that are signs for those who reflect. (30:21)

O Mary! Behold, God has elected thee and made thee pure, and raised thee above all the women of the world. (3:42)

Diversity/Peace/Interfaith

For every one of you have We designated a law and a way of life. And if God had so willed, He could surely have made you all one single community: But He willed it otherwise in order to test you by means of what He has bestowed on you. Strive, then, with one another in doing good! Your goal is God; and then, He will make you understand the truth of everything in which you have differed. (5:48)

Repel [evil] with what is better: Then will he between whom and thee was hatred become as it were thy friend and intimate! (41:34)

The servants of the Infinitely Compassionate One are those who walk on the Earth in humility, and when the ignorant address them they say, "Peace!" (25:63)

O humankind! We created you all out of a male and a female, and made you into nations and tribes that you might know each other. (49:13)

We believe in Allah, and the revelation given to us, and to Abraham, Ismail, Isaac, Jacob, and the descendants [children of Jacob] and that given to Moses and Jesus and that given to [all] prophets from their Lord: We make no difference between one and another of them.   (2:136)

O Mary! Behold, God sends thee the glad tiding, through a word from Him, [of a son] who shall become known as the Christ Jesus, son of Mary, of great honor in this world and in the life to come, and [shall be] of those who are drawn near unto God.
                                                                    (3:45)

Mystery and Passage

And of everything, We have created opposites that you might bear in mind that God alone is one.   (51:49)

I am He and He is I, except that I am I and He is He.   (HADITH)

I was a secret treasure and I longed to be known. So I created the worlds, visible and invisible.   (HADITH)

And if all the trees on Earth were pens, and the sea [were ink], with seven [more] seas yet added to it, the words of God would not be exhausted.   (31:27)

It is better to blush in this world than in the next.   (HADITH)

When you were born, everyone was laughing but you were crying. Live your life so that when you die, everyone is crying, but you are laughing.   (HADITH)

To Allah we belong and to Him is our return.   (2:156)

O soul in complete rest and satisfaction! Return to your Sustainer well-pleased and well-pleasing! Enter then among my devoted ones! Yes, enter my Garden!   (89:27–28)

THE MOST BEAUTIFUL NAMES
OF ALLAH: *ASMA AL-HUSNA*

Allah		The Greatest Name
Ar-Rahman	1	The All-Merciful
Ar-Rahim	2	The All-Beneficent
Al-Malik	3	The Absolute Ruler
Al-Quddus	4	The Pure One
As-Salam	5	The Source of Peace
Al-Mu'min	6	The Inspirer of Faith
Al-Muhaymin	7	The Guardian
Al-'Aziz	8	The Victorious
Al-Jabbar	9	The Compeller
Al-Mutakabbir	10	The Greatest
Al-Khaliq	11	The Creator
Al-Bari'	12	The Maker of Order
Al-Musawwir	13	The Shaper of Beauty
Al-Ghaffar	14	The Forgiving
Al-Qahhar	15	The Subduer
Al-Wahhab	16	The Giver of All
Ar-Razzaq	17	The Sustainer
Al-Fattah	18	The Opener

Al-'Alim	19	The Knower of All
Al-Qabid	20	The Constrictor
Al-Basit	21	The Reliever
Al-Khafid	22	The Abaser
Ar-Rafi'	23	The Exalter
Al-Mu'izz	24	The Bestower of Honors
Al-Mudhill	25	The Humiliator
As-Sami	26	The Hearer of All
Al-Basir	27	The Seer of All
Al-Hakam	28	The Judge
Al-'Adl	29	The Just
Al-Latif	30	The Subtle One
Al-Khabir	31	The All-Aware
Al-Halim	32	The Forebearing
Al-'Azim	33	The Magnificent
Al-Ghafur	34	The Forgiver and Hider of Faults
Ash-Shakur	35	The Rewarder of Thankfulness
Al-'Ali	36	The Highest
Al-Kabir	37	The Greatest
Al-Hafiz	38	The Preserver
Al-Muqit	39	The Nourisher
Al-Hasib	40	The Accounter
Al-Jalil	41	The Mighty
Al-Karim	42	The Generous
Ar-Raqib	43	The Watchful One
Al-Mujib	44	The Responder to Prayer
Al-Wasi'	45	The All-Comprehending
Al-Hakim	46	The Perfectly Wise
Al-Wadud	47	The Loving One
Al-Majíd	48	The Majestic One

Al-Ba'ith	49	The Resurrector
Ash-Shahid	50	The Witness
Al-Haqq	51	The Truth
Al-Wakil	52	The Trustee
Al-Qawi	53	The Possessor of All Strength
Al-Matin	54	The Forceful One
Al-Wáli	55	The Governor
Al-Hamid	56	The Praised One
Al-Muhsi	57	The Appraiser
Al-Mubdi	58	The Originator
Al-Mu'id	59	The Restorer
Al-Muhyi	60	The Giver of Life
Al-Mumit	61	The Taker of Life
Al-Hayy	62	The Ever Living One
Al-Qayyum	63	The Self-Existing One
Al-Wajid	64	The Finder
Al-Májid	65	The Glorious
Al-Wahid	66	The Only One
Al-Ahad	67	The One
As-Samad	68	The Satisfier of All Needs
Al-Qadir	69	The All Powerful
Al-Muqtadir	70	The Creator of All Power
Al-Muqaddim	71	The Expediter
Al-Mu'akhkhir	72	The Delayer
Al-Awwal	73	The First
Al-Akhir	74	The Last
Az-Zahir	75	The Manifest One
Al-Batin	76	The Hidden One
Al-Walí	77	The Protecting Friend
Al-Muta'ali	78	The Supreme One

Al-Barr	79	The Doer of Good
At-Tawwab	80	The Guide to Repentance
Al-Muntaqim	81	The Avenger
Al-Afu	82	The Forgiver
Ar-Ra'uf	83	The Clement
Malik al-Mulk	84	The Owner of All
Dhul-Jalali Wal-Ikram	85	The Lord of Majesty and Bounty
Al-Muqsit	86	The Equitable One
Al-Jami	87	The Gatherer
Al-Ghani	88	The Rich One
Al-Mughni	89	The Enricher
Al-Mani'	90	The Preventer of Harm
Ad-Darr	91	The Creator of the Harmful
An-Nafi	92	The Creator of Good
An-Nur	93	The Light
Al-Hadi	94	The Guide
Al-Badi	95	The Originator
Al-Baqi	96	The Everlasting One
Al-Warith	97	The Inheritor of All
Ar-Rashid	98	The Righteous Teacher
As-Sabur	99	The Patient One

The Most Beautiful Names, by Tosun Bayrak al-Jerrahi al-Halveti

BIBLIOGRAPHY AND
SUGGESTIONS FOR
FURTHER READING

Barks, Coleman. *The Essential Rumi*. New York: HarperCollins, 1997.

Cleary, Thomas. *Living and Dying with Grace: Counsels of Hadrat Ali*. Boston: Shambhala, 1996.

Frager, Robert. *Heart, Self and Soul: The Sufi Psychology of Growth, Balance and Harmony*. Wheaton, IL: Theosophical Publishing House, 1999.

Helminski, Camille. *The Book of Character: Writings on Character and Virtue from Islamic and Other Sources*. Watsonville, CA: The Book Foundation, 2004.

Helminski, Camille, and Kabir Helminski. *Jewels of Remembrance: A Daybook of Spiritual Guidance Containing 365 Selections from the Wisdom of Mevlana Jalaluddin Rumi*. Putney, VT: Threshold Books, 1996.

———. *Rumi Daylight: A Daybook of Spiritual Guidance*. Boston: Shambhala, 1999.

Houston, Jean. *The Search for the Beloved: Journeys in Mythology and Sacred Psychology*. New York: Tarcher, 1997.

———. *The Gift: Poems by Hafiz the Great Sufi Master*. New York: Penguin, 1999.

Ladinsky, Daniel. *Love Poems from God: Twelve Sacred Voices from the East and West*. New York: Penguin, 2002.

Llewellyn, Vaughan-Lee. *Sufism: The Transformation of the Heart*. San Francisco: The Golden Sufi Center, 1995.

Rahman, Jamal. *The Fragrance of Faith: The Enlightened Heart of Islam.* Watsonville, CA: The Book Foundation, 2004.

Rahman, Jamal, Don Mackenzie, and Ted Falcon. *Getting to the Heart of Interfaith: The Eye-Opening, Hope-Filled Friendship of a Pastor, a Rabbi & an Imam.* Woodstock, VT: SkyLight Paths, 2009.

———. *Religion Gone Astray: What We Found at the Heart of Interfaith.* Woodstock, VT: SkyLight Paths, 2011.

Rahman, Jamal, Kathleen Schmit Elias, and Ann Holmes Redding. *Out of Darkness into Light: Spiritual Guidance in the Quran with Reflections from Jewish and Christian Scriptures.* New York: Morehouse, 2009.

Sis, Peter. *The Conference of the Birds.* New York: Penguin Press, 2011.

Starr, Mirabai. *God of Love: A Guide to the Heart of Judaism, Christianity and Islam.* Rhinebeck, NY: Monkfish, 2012.

About SKYLIGHT PATHS Publishing

SkyLight Paths Publishing is creating a place where people of different spiritual traditions come together for challenge and inspiration, a place where we can help each other understand the mystery that lies at the heart of our existence.

Through spirituality, our religious beliefs are increasingly becoming a part of our lives—rather than *apart* from our lives. While many of us may be more interested than ever in spiritual growth, we may be less firmly planted in traditional religion. Yet, we do want to deepen our relationship to the sacred, to learn from our own as well as from other faith traditions, and to practice in new ways.

SkyLight Paths sees both believers and seekers as a community that increasingly transcends traditional boundaries of religion and denomination—people wanting to learn from each other, *walking together, finding the way.*

For your information and convenience, at the back of this book we have provided a list of other SkyLight Paths books you might find interesting and useful. They cover the following subjects:

Buddhism / Zen	Global Spiritual	Monasticism
Catholicism	Perspectives	Mysticism
Children's Books	Gnosticism	Poetry
Christianity	Hinduism /	Prayer
Comparative	Vedanta	Religious Etiquette
Religion	Inspiration	Retirement
Current Events	Islam / Sufism	Spiritual Biography
Earth-Based	Judaism	Spiritual Direction
Spirituality	Kabbalah	Spirituality
Enneagram	Meditation	Women's Interest
	Midrash Fiction	Worship

Printed in the USA
CPSIA information can be obtained
at www.ICGtesting.com
JSHW021604110923
48261JS00002B/5